PRINCIPLE
PREACHING

PRINCIPLE
PREACHING

How to Create and Deliver Purpose Driven® Sermons
FOR LIFE APPLICATIONS

JOHN R. BISAGNO

BROADMAN
&HOLMAN
PUBLISHERS

NASHVILLE, TENNESSEE

0–8054–2454–7

Published by Broadman & Holman Publishers,
Nashville, Tennessee

Category: PREACHING

1 2 3 4 5 6 7 8 9 10 07 06 05 04 03 02

To my beautiful wife

Uldine

whose very life is a sermon

CONTENTS

PART 3: Principles from New Testament Characters

Part 1
The Basics of Principle Preaching

CHAPTER 1

Learning to Preach
the Principle Way

Pastor Rick Warren of Saddleback Community Church in Mission Viejo, California, among others, has been espousing a "new kind" of preaching. On the surface, it is extremely simple. In fact, its impact is most profound. It is called *principle preaching*. Principle preaching reduced to its simplest definition is drawing life application principles from the Bible and preaching them as the outline of the sermon. In each case, the three or four or even five divisions of the sermon are principles, not the usual sermon points.

Most pastors preach a sermon outline that is really rather predictable. The points usually contain life application principles, though not identified primarily as such. But in principle preaching, the principles themselves *are* the points. The normal sermon outline, which merely contains principles, is customarily more for the preacher's sake than the hearer's.

In principle preaching, the hearer has an instant connection and virtually never forgets what he or she has heard. A sermon outline with three or four principles will cause listeners to write them down, magnet them to the refrigerator door and say, "Now, I can do that when I get to work tomorrow." In principle preaching, the principles themselves are the outline, not simply truths contained in a rather predictable, customary talk. Outlines are soon forgotten, but principles never are.

The power of principle preaching is simple. Principles are universally applicable. Thus, receptivity is accordingly universal. If it is true in physics that everything that goes up must come down, it is also true in principle preaching, where virtually every principle will be heard, received, remembered, practiced, and even perpetuated by those who hear the Word. Whether one is saved or lost, a communist or Catholic, a Buddhist or Baptist, an astronaut, truck driver, banker, or custodian, the principles will stick.

Certainly principle preaching will not be the exclusive vehicle by which preachers deliver God's Word. Funerals, for example, call for brief and tender words of comfort in Scripture with virtually no outline at all. Weddings, evangelistic crusades, and a host of other venues call for their own styles of outline, content, and delivery.

Word-by-word teaching deepens the understanding of God's people, and it should be the mid-week approach when deeper Bible study for the faithful is undertaken. But bring some principle preaching to your congregation. They will be richly blessed and will actually remember what you preached.

Would you like to see an example of how to draw life application principles for a sermon from a memorable experience in the life of the man chosen by God to be Moses' successor? Let's look at one now.

CHAPTER 2

The Call of Joshua

Joshua 1:1–7

The average sermon outline on this passage might typically be something like this:

1. The Call of Joshua
2. The Command of Joshua
3. The Conquest of Joshua
4. The Courage of Joshua

The able pastor can make a few good life applications within the framework of this traditional outline. What often happens, though, is that listeners lose interest because the outline contains merely predictable points, rather than life changing principles. A principle preacher might outline the same passage of Scripture as follows:

1. Don't Get Stuck in Life's Passageways (Josh. 1:1–2).

Life is like a mansion. Many of us spend our life in the hallways, stuck between the big room of a regrettable yesterday from which we cannot get free and the fantasy of the large room of a tomorrow to which we are going. Many of the persons I know seem to be going nowhere. They are stuck somewhere between a yesterday that enslaves them and the fantasy of a tomorrow onto which they cannot grab. Life is like that, and too many of us are frozen between potential experiences that beckon us and the memories that enslave us.

5

After the death of Moses, God said bluntly to Joshua, "Moses my servant is dead. Stand up and lead this people forward." Perhaps the most obvious difference between emotional, mental, and spiritual maturity and a lack of it is the ability or inability to live in a world where a thousand escape mechanisms beckon to us. God strongly pressed Joshua into reality. "Moses is dead. Life goes on. Stand up. Go forward." God gives us tears to weep, but not forever. He allows our hearts to break, but not indefinitely. There is almost a sternness in the text as God says to his servant, "Life goes on. Face reality. The man is dead. The job is yours. Get on with it."

2. God's Already Been Where You're Going (Josh. 1:3).

Fear of tomorrow can be as crippling as slavery to the past, but God is already in your tomorrow. He's already been where you're going. Child of God, do not fear what lies ahead. He holds the future, and He holds you in His hand. God has gone before you and secured tomorrow on your behalf. Notice God does not say, "Everywhere your foot shall trod I *will* give you," but rather, "I *have* given unto you." He's already done it. With God, there's no yesterday, today, and tomorrow. He not only sees the beginning and the end, He *is* the beginning and the end. Tomorrow is already today with God. Don't be afraid to walk into it.

3. God Has a Wonderful Blueprint for Your Life (Josh. 1:4).

God is in every detail. He has prepared all things for you and they will work together for your good. Our Lord has left nothing to chance. He is never surprised or caught off guard. He is a sovereign God who has carefully planned a beautiful life for you. He who loves you more than you know has left nothing to chance. What a perfect blueprint God outlines! He promised Joshua vast territory on every side—from the desert to Lebanon, to the great Euphrates River, all the land of the Hittites, all the way to the great sea where the sun sets in the west.

God also outlines the north, south, east, and west borders of your life. God's will is going to be done in your life if you love Him, trust Him, and go forward. He has prepared everything specifically for you so that all things will work together for your good.

4. Yesterday's Faithfulness Guarantees Tomorrow's Courage (Josh. 1:5–7).

God will be with you, just as He was with Moses. He will never leave you nor forsake you. He will prosper you wherever you go. How could young Joshua be confident and courageous in the challenge of tomorrow? The answer lies in God's faithfulness Joshua had observed in the life of Moses yesterday. What He has done, He will do. Be strong and be encouraged.

The text, of course, continues, and the principles are endless, but this example models the power of principle preaching. Ninety-nine percent of your hearers will have forgotten by next Sunday that you talked about the call, command, conquest, and courage of Joshua; but they will never forget God's great principles as they apply to their own lives.

CHAPTER 3

Principle Preaching from Topics

The great narratives of both Old and New Testament best lend themselves to principle preaching, but it is also possible to preach sermons with principles that will not be forgotten from topics, as well as from narrative. The reservoir of potential topics for principle preaching is inexhaustible.

Every topic under heaven is a ready subject for exciting biblical principle preaching. "Starting Over" offers a good example of principle preaching from a topic. The turn of a new century, decade, or even new year is a wonderful opportunity to encourage people to get rid of the past and begin anew. Anything that helps our hearers do this is of great value.

Virtually each of us carries emotional baggage. A neighbor abused me, a boss fired me, a teacher failed me, a friend lied about me, a spouse was unfaithful to me, or may have even divorced me. In addition, how often do these childhood tapes, or ones like them, replay in our minds: "Why can't you be like your sister?" or "You'll never amount to anything."

Many of us suffer from an unforgiving spirit rooted in bitterness toward another person who may even be deceased. Your refusal to forgive may not be hurting anyone else, but its physiological, psychological, and emotional harm will probably send you to an early grave and may cause physical and emotional illness.

There's no way to overstate the importance of "letting it go." At the conclusion of the Lord's Prayer, Jesus emphasized just one thing He had said: "But if you don't forgive people, your Father will not forgive your wrongdoing" (Matt. 6:15). Notice that Jesus uses the word "forgive" twice in the same sentence, underscoring its importance. Does this mean God's forgiveness is somehow based on a human work I must perform, rather than on the free gift of His grace? Certainly not. God grants His gracious favor on the basis of no human work, but upon His marvelous grace. It does mean that if I cannot forgive, I will never be in an attitude to humble myself before the Lord Jesus and ask His forgiveness. My unwillingness to forgive is an indication of a prideful spirit which must yet be nailed to the cross.

So important is letting it go that Jesus said, "If you come to worship and remember someone has something against you, leave your gift at the altar, go settle the issue, and then come and worship." Notice that He did not say, "If you have something against another," rather, "If they have something against you." So important are human relationships as an expression of our right relationship with God that even if we have done no wrong but another has wronged us, we are still to initiate the process of reconciliation. Bitterness, hatred, and unforgiveness must not be dragged into the future. A principle outline of a topical sermon on "letting it go" might look like this:

1. Letting It Go Is a Choice You Make, Not Because It Feels Right, but Because It Is Right.

Often we hear others say, "I cannot forgive him because he hurt me so badly." What they mean is, "I cannot voluntarily commit to forgiveness because I cannot emotionally get over the hurt." But forgiving and forgetting can never be done emotionally until they are first done voluntarily.

We say, "If I felt it, I would act," but Scripture teaches, "If we act it, we will feel it." In the third chapter of Philippians, Paul acknowledges his struggle to become everything Christ intended when He reached out and touched Paul's life. The apostle reminds us that we must concentrate total focus and unrestrained energy on dealing with the past before progress can be made in the journey toward tomorrow. How power-ful is his declaration, "But one thing I do." What is the one main thing he has committed to do? To forget those things that are behind, as verse 13 tells us.

In the second chapter of Revelation, Jesus the Bridegroom reprimands the Ephesian church, His bride, for falling out of love with Him. In the three-point prescription for her sick-ness, He tells her, "Remember, repent, and do." Not a word of emotion is in this passage. There is nothing the bride is told to feel, but there are three things she is told to do: Remember, repent, and do again her first works; in other words, she is to act as she once did. It is in the doing that emotion thrives.

David is a marvelous example of a conscious choice to let go of the past. After the birth of his son, David lay prostrate on the floor fasting and praying for eight days and nights, pleading with God for his son's life. God chose not to answer David's prayer. When the servants told him, "The baby is dead," David did not rise up in anger, curse God, and refuse to be consoled; but as a mature believer, he made the choice to go on with his life. Second Samuel 12:20 says, "Then David got up from the ground. After he had washed, put on lotions and changed his clothes, he went into the house of the LORD and worshiped. Then he went to his own house, and at his request they served him food, and he ate."

As human beings, we consist of three parts:

• The mind—the seat of knowledge, where we know
• The heart—the seat of emotion, where we feel
• The soul—the seat of the will, where we commit

Turning loose of the past is never possible in the realm of the emotion. If you wait until you feel like forgiving, you will never forgive and will suffer the consequences. Forgiving is a choice of the will that you make in your soul.

2. Remember That God Is Not Accountable to Us, but We Are Accountable to Him.

Beneath the fruit of an unforgiving spirit is often a root of bitterness and anger against God. Truth be told, many of us have never come to terms with the fact that we are really angry at God, whom we feel could have prevented the catastrophe but did not. Casting blame on God for human acts has its beginnings early in human nature. Adam essentially blamed God for his fall when he said, "The woman you put here with me—she gave me some fruit from the tree, and I ate it" (Gen. 3:12). The inference is clear: "God, it's really your fault. Had you not given me this woman, she could not have given me this apple and I would not be in this fix."

Let me tell you one of the saddest stories I know. A man in East Texas lost a very successful business due to the oil bust of the mid-1980s. Forced to move to Houston and start again, both he and his wife took new jobs—he as a gas station attendant and she as a secretary. In the office, she met a man, had an affair, and divorced a loving husband. Today he is still angry at God. How often have I heard him say, "Had God prevented the price of oil from going down, this economic tragedy never would have occurred; we never would have moved to Houston, and I would never have lost my wife. God, it's your fault."

Perhaps you never have identified it, let alone articulated it, but just beneath your bitterness toward another person may be a layer of bitterness toward God, whom you blame for allowing it to happen in the first place.

After Job's great loss, his wife said, "Curse God and die." Job's answer was, "Shall I take good at the hand of God and not ill as well?"

It is often said the purpose of the book of Job is to answer the question, "Why do the righteous suffer?" But the book ends without answering that question. The purpose of Job may well be to say that you don't have to know why you suffer. Job affirmed, "Though He slay me, yet will I trust Him." His was the mature response to the suffering of a believer.

Scripture does not promise we will ever know why we suffer here. Surely in heaven we will understand, for we shall know as we are known. But until then, the issue is not God's explanation to us, but our response to Him. Never does our light shine as brightly to the glory of God as against the backdrop of our darkest hour of suffering.

3. Nothing Anyone Has Done to You Can Compare with What You Have Done to God.

When it seems impossible to forgive another, remember how much greater wrong has been forgiven you. For one sinner to sin against another is a relatively minor thing, but to sin against a holy God is an unfathomable thing. If God has forgiven you so much, then whatever you forgive against a fellow sinner is relatively small.

In the eighteenth chapter of Matthew, Jesus tells the story of an unjust steward. A servant was forgiven a debt of ten thousand talents by his king, whose compassion spared him and his family the humiliation of imprisonment and slavery. The forgiven man found a fellow servant who owed him a hundred denarii, but the forgiven one refused to forgive his brother and cast him into prison with his family. The king was so angry that he cast the man who would not forgive into outer darkness. Could it be that a man who will not forgive goes to hell? Could it be that one who does not understand forgiveness has never been to the cross and knows not our Lord at all? When you have trouble letting it go, just remember that you, too, are a sinner, and that nothing your fellow sinner has done to you can compare with your sin against a righteous and holy God.

4. Focus Not on What You Have Lost but on What You Have Left.

When the elder brother complained that the father had killed one calf from his herd to feed the penitent prodigal, the father replied, "Son, everything I have is yours." All the cattle, herds, and flocks belonged to that elder brother. How could he have been so bitter over the loss of one head of cattle when hundreds or even thousands remained? The elder son's anger seemed to center on the father's welcoming home the prodigal. But the father's loving response indicates a deeper problem he knew all too well.

It is indeed possible to act our way into new thinking when we voluntarily choose to let it go. And we reinforce that commitment when we also choose to think our way into new actions. The father's plea to the elder brother was, "Son, forget about one lost calf and rejoice in a thousand unlost cattle." The apostle Paul reminds us, "Whatsoever things are lovely, virtuous, pure and of good report, if there be any virtue, if there be any praise, think on *these* things."

Learn to focus on what you have left, rather than on what you lost. Perhaps it was a job, a possession, or even a precious child, but you may well be letting your unresolved bitterness so negatively affect you that you are damaging the spiritual and emotional health of those close to you. Focus on the great people they are. If you have the Lord, your family, and your health, little else matters. Rejoice!

CHAPTER 4

Principle Preaching
and the Expositor

Principle preaching need not be shallow preaching. It is, in fact, in the best sense of the word, *expository* preaching. After each principle in a sermon, you state what you have said, apply it to the life, and illustrate it to the heart. Pastor Rick Warren aptly outlines these steps:

1. State the principle.
2. Explain the principle.
3. Apply the principle.
4. Illustrate the principle.

The primary emphasis on each principle is its explanation. What is expository preaching if not the exposition of truth? And what is exposition if not the discipline of exposing the depth of the text, revealing its meaning, and explaining how it applies to one's life? The finest hermeneutic one can employ must be brought to bear upon the explanation of the stated principle, for herein is the light of understanding and the lamp of transformation to the heart.

Remember the plan: state the principle, explain the principle, apply the principle, and illustrate the principle. Clearly, you should spend the most time in explaining the principle that comes from the text. So profound is the impact of a life-application principle, you need do little more to make it stick than to state it. It is in identifying, explaining, and illustrating the principle that the major work of a creative principle preacher needs to be done. You need to do far less to apply the principle to the life of the hearer. Here more than anywhere else the Holy Spirit convicts the heart of the hearer to how the principle applies to his life. As expositor, you will assist, but here, more than anywhere, the Holy Spirit does His work of application. Every Scripture has only one correct interpretation, but it may have a million applications. Regardless of how you apply it, the Holy Spirit will go beyond your words and explicitly apply it to the unique needs of each individual listener.

The story that illustrates the principle must always be relevant and fresh, something to which the hearer will instantly relate. Throw away those old illustration books and read *USA Today, Time, Newsweek, People* and a major daily newspaper, and regularly view local and national newscasts. Antiques are for decorating homes, not sermons. Employing every hermeneutical and homiletical device at your disposal reinforces the principle you are preaching. Use everything you learn in seminary. Synthesize the text. Interpret the Greek or Hebrew. Define the context. Set the rich historical background.

I say again, principle preaching is not by definition shallow preaching. The principle sermon will contain the same amount of exposition you learned in classrooms in homiletics and hermeneutics and used in your previous expository sermons. But set the exposition in a context of developing principles that state, exegete, explain, and illustrate, and watch your congregation open their minds and hearts to God's truth as a rose to the morning sun. Even more importantly, watch them take what they understand and now remember and translate it into victorious living.

As we journey through the pages that follow, we shall set forth in each story (whether you use it for personal devotion, Sunday school lessons, or sermons) life principles you can state, explain, apply, and illustrate with a life-changing purpose in view.

While we strongly affirm the guidelines of Pastor Warren to state, explain, apply, and illustrate the principle, it is important the principle sermonizer remember to employ the craft more as an *artist* than as a *mechanic*. "One, two, three, four, and out" on every principle may itself dictate a predictability that is counterproductive. While generally following these four guidelines, the principle sermonizer will be open to the creative and artistic freedom of the Holy Spirit, who made not even two snowflakes just alike.

CHAPTER 5

Preaching from Bible Characters

I have selected one story or idea from each of forty-seven Bible personalities. Perhaps future works will expand, offering many more principle sermons on each. My prayer is that your creative juices may be stirred as we banquet on the inexhaustible truths of His Word and dine at the table of life-impact principles just begging to be noticed, principles that burst from every incident in the life of every character in virtually every chapter of the Bible. Happy dining!

Let's digest tidbits of stories from some of the greatest lives ever lived and find principles that have impacted millions across the centuries. Ask God for a creative heart. See beneath the surface. Put yourselves in the skin of these people and ask, "Why did they do what they did? What were they really thinking that they didn't say? Why did the Holy Spirit preserve just this?" Try to go beyond what the story says to what it *is*—about you, about me, about life.

God loves creativity. He's the author of art and beauty, sculpture and music, drama and poetry and painting. Ours is a creative, artistic God. No two persons are just alike, no two sunsets the same. There are creative powers inside you that you may have never used. Ask God to enhance them by His Holy Spirit, and think with me; think of the treasure of great principles that lie beneath the sand of the surface in each story.

The Old Testament portrays many persons whose lives teach us about God and ourselves:

Adam	Moses	Saul
Eve	Pharaoh	David
Noah	Joshua	Jonathan
Abraham	Elijah	Bathsheba
Sarah	Elisha	Esther
Isaac	Gideon	Daniel
Jacob	Samson	Jonah
Joseph	Ruth	

The New Testament offers a number of additional persons worthy of examination:

Mary	Martha	Luke
Joseph	Woman with the	John the Apostle
John the Baptist	Issue of Blood	Simon the Sorcerer
Matthew	Woman at the	Paul
Demoniac of	Well	Barnabas
Gadara	Woman Taken in	Lydia
Peter	Adultery	Aquila and Priscilla
Andrew	Judas	Timothy
Mary Magdalene	Pilate	Demas

We shall attempt here no finished product, just a touch of background and an occasional story. The emphasis is to get you into the mindset of creativity, finding the principles God gives you. These chapters will stimulate your imagination and challenge you to flesh them out and expand them into your own special God-breathed sermon. Little, if any, exposition is done here. The focus will be on learning to find and develop the principles.

Principle Preaching is certainly not the only way to preach, but I urge you to learn to tap your creativity and add this new way of preaching to your Gospel arsenal. You will find your audience relating in an entirely new way.

Part 2
Principles from
Old Testament Characters

CHAPTER 6

Adam

Genesis 2:15–17; 3:1–4, 9

1. God's Boundaries Equate to Our Freedom.

Why boundaries? Could it be God established boundaries for Adam and Eve in order to provide them with ultimate freedom and the ability to choose it? Throughout history wars have been fought over the right to make choices, yet God provided that gift to man at creation. It was an act of love and great risk on the part of our Creator, who wanted us to choose Him and His plan for our lives. God knew something we often forget: Real freedom is not simply the right to rebel. Real freedom only comes through discipline. The stop signs of life are there to give each of us the freedom to cross the intersection in safety. One who obeys the rules will be free to drive another day. Romans 6:16 reminds us that freedom isn't free. We must choose to be servants of sin or servants of righteousness.

Our culture is crazy about games and sports, and in every sport there are established boundaries. Referees blow a whistle or throw a flag, and play comes to a halt. They call a penalty and impose a consequence. Leagues go to great lengths to make the playing field fair for all who participate. Instant replay attempts to determine whether the receiver was in bounds or out of bounds. Improved technology attempts to protect the integrity of the game. Can you imagine your favorite sport without any rules? The result would be chaos, and there would be no pleasure in the game. Certainly sports are not life, despite what Madison Avenue would suggest, but the boundaries God established at creation are even more important than the width of a football field or the out-of-bounds marker on a golf course. Boundaries protect us and are God's established guides to lead us to Him.

Study the past and discover the importance of protective boundaries. Ask the people of Jericho about the protection provided by the wall around their city. Consider the work of Nehemiah and the children of Israel as they rebuilt the wall around Jerusalem. Our culture has bought in to the idea that boundaries are for punishment, not protection, but nothing could be farther from the truth. Our Heavenly Father, who loves us with an everlasting love, established boundaries for Adam and Eve at creation because He knew if they did not learn to make wise choices, they would never choose Him.

Have you ever played a board game with one of your children? Little ones with a strong need to succeed often decide to make up rules as the game progresses. When my daughter was young, she would invent rules on the spot. Of course, the new rules were always designed to favor her. When confronted about the rules she would simply declare, "It's my game and I make the rules." If she really got angry, she would just quit the game. The latest Jack in the Box restaurants' slogan says, "The holidays aren't over until I say they're over." Sadly, many adults go through life trying to erase the boundaries and adjust the rules to improve their position. But God, the best parent ever, will not let us get away with it. His boundaries are as eternal as His love.

2. The Freedom to Choose Demands Responsibility for the Choice.

Every privilege carries with it a responsibility, and the greater the privilege the greater the responsibility. A driver's license can be revoked for failure to follow the rules, and the privilege of using a credit card can be canceled when the bills are not paid. Freedom of choice makes man in the image of God and sets him apart from the animal kingdom. But with the privilege of choice comes personal responsibility for one's actions. Basic to human personhood is moral choice, and it is the very heart of the Judeo-Christian faith. Responsibility for one's actions, moral choices, and subsequent consequences of blessing or pain are the exclusive privileges of those created in the image of God.

Parents have the awesome privilege of raising their children to be responsible adults. The process is both educational and experiential, and wise parents gradually give children the privilege of making their own choices based on their age and level of maturity. Do you remember the first time you allowed your child to ride a bicycle around the block? My wife and I counted the minutes and watched with great apprehension as our son made his maiden two-wheel voyage; but it had to be done, even at the risk of disaster. God gave Adam and Eve a wide range of responsibilities in the garden and only one prohibition. When they failed with that privilege, He held them accountable, as would any loving parent with their child.

We are all accountable to God for what we do and the choices we make. Archibald Hart defines accountability as encouragement, and that's exactly what happened when God came to confront Adam and Eve in their sin. Even though they had failed and were suffering the consequences, God provided for their needs by making garments for them and establishing new boundaries. He loves us enough to hold us to a holy standard, and He directs us in the way He has planned for our lives.

3. Partial Truth Is No Truth at All.

The cornerstone of all quality life is truth. Truth, without any mixture of error, is absolutely essential to life. Whether in marriage or mathematics, social behavior or sexual mores, partial truth is no truth at all.

Satan's first approach to Eve was a classic example of how he works and a pattern from which he never varies, and it happened in spite of the influence of Adam. His approach was not "God has not said," rather "Did God really say that?" He did not call God's Word untrue. He simply raised the doubt. Are you sure it is true? It was only as Eve reeled beneath the staggering possibility God's Word might not be true, that he spoke the lie, "You will not surely die." It was a very short mental journey from "Are you sure of God's Word?" to "You cannot be sure of God's Word." Satan is the master of the subtle attack. Seldom does he come with a frontal assault on truth. Partial truth, half-truths, and deception are his constant ploy; and the first man and woman would be the first to learn this bitter lesson.

Two of the great questions in life are: "Can I trust God?" and "Can God trust me?" The issue in the garden was a question of trust. Did God really mean what He said? If He does, can you trust that it is best for your life? The question has not changed down through the years. Remember the old television show, *Father Knows Best?* Our Heavenly Father definitely knows what is best. He never makes an error in judgment as He lays out the plan for each of our lives.

Continuously though, there is our adversary, seeking to convince us we really know what is best for our lives. Every person must confront the questions "In whom shall I believe?" and "On what shall I base my life?" God is very clear here. His Word is absolute truth, and it does not change with the times or fluctuate based on the latest polls. Down through the ages countless millions have concluded God can be trusted. Once that decision is reached, the question becomes: "Can God trust me?" He believes He can, so much that He has offered freedom of choice as a gift to each of us, and no completely right choices can be made on incomplete truth.

4. The Head Has Full Responsibility for the Whole.

With the mantle of leadership comes the responsibility for those following in one's footsteps. In the home, in the church, in business, in government, it is always true. In Genesis 2:10–17, God told Adam the rules. You may be sure that Adam passed them on to Eve. In Genesis 3:2–3, we read that she knows precisely what God told her husband. But Eve was alone when Satan tempted her. Away from the protection of her husband, Satan found her a vulnerable prey. Genesis 3:6 says both Adam and Eve ate. They both made inadequate provision for their sin. They both heard the voice of God. But when God came in judgment, it was Adam, and Adam alone, whom He held accountable for the actions of his family. He asked in verse 9, "Adam, where are you?" And in verse 11, "Who told you that you were naked?" He also asked the man, "Have you eaten of the tree that I commanded you not to eat from?"

Adam's response has been repeated throughout history. He invented the Blame Game. It's more popular than Monopoly. We all play it. When confronted with our sin, we shift the focus, and look for a likely candidate to take the fall. In Adam's case there were not a lot of candidates, but he found one. Since God was responsible for putting Eve in the garden, surely He must accept some of the blame. But God would not let Adam play the Blame Game, and He put the responsibility right back in his lap. Adam was the leader, and he must shoulder the burden for the sin committed.

Scapegoats are popular in our society. Somehow we feel better if we can find someone to blame when our team doesn't win or our stocks don't soar. We fire and then we hire, in hopes the next leader will be more successful. Our politicians have learned to spin everything since they are more difficult to fire. Failed marriages demand a scapegoat, but divorce is still easy and popular. Some states have no-fault divorce, attempting to spare both parties the indignity of admitting their part in the ending of a marriage. All of this, and more, means no one wants to accept responsibility for the consequences of their actions. Nowhere is unwillingness to accept responsibility for one's behavior than is found in the lame excuse of the homosexual community, "But it's in my genes—I was born this way."

But God has always demanded acceptance of responsibility from His leaders. Moses paid the price of not taking it—God did not allow him to enter the Promised Land. David was confronted in his sin by the prophet Nathan. Jonah was swallowed by the great fish. Saul was struck down and blinded on the road to Damascus. Leadership means not that one will never make mistakes, but that one must acknowledge them and accept the consequences.

Life went on for Adam and Eve, though their lives would change forever. Adam learned what it meant to be a leader. It was not a responsibility he chose, but one God assigned him. What are the responsibilities in your life? Have you accepted them? Are you willing to assume the God-given role you have been assigned? God promises to give you wisdom and discernment for the journey, and all you have to do is ask.

CHAPTER 7

Eve

Genesis 3:1–6

1. God Always Holds Back Something for Himself.

Ours is a gracious God. He gives and gives and gives again. His manifold goodness is legendary, His grace and provision inexhaustible. And yet there are boundaries. The number one theme of Scripture is salvation; the second is stewardship. Thirty-two of Jesus' thirty-six parables are about a man's relationship to his possessions. In each one the message is that God is the owner and that we are only the managers, the temporary stewards, over God's world.

Webster defines a steward as "one who manages the assets and affairs of another." As gracious as is our God, the owner/creator, with His creation, He never shares everything with the manager. No owner does that.

The Bible is filled with example after example of this principle in action. After six days of creation, God said, "Rest on the seventh day. That's my day." In the Promised Land, God said, "Let the land rest every seventh year. That's my year. That's the time for you to meditate on who sends the sun and rain and who makes the harvest grow."

In the garden, God provided for every human need. Thousands of plants and trees provided Adam and Eve with the source of perfect health. He created Adam and Eve as vegetarians. "Freely eat," God said. "Enjoy, enjoy. However," the Lord continued, "there is one tree from which you cannot eat. That's my tree (the tree of the knowledge of good and evil).

I reserve it for myself. You may not touch it. You may not eat of it or you will die." But they did—and they did.

Some might read the story of Adam and Eve in the garden and believe that God set them up to fail. Quite the contrary, God knows that giving is learned behavior. I've never seen giving parents raise selfish children. Just as it is important for parents to model giving for our children, God knew that as our Heavenly Father, He needed to set the example for us. By providing everything Adam and Eve could possibly need, He established a foundation from which they could learn the joys of giving back and the importance of obedience.

Have you learned this principle? Unfortunately, most have not. Sit down with your calendar and your canceled checks at the end of a year. Take a look at where your money and your time have been spent. Ask yourself this question: "Was it worth it?" God has modeled giving for each of us in many ways, and our response should be instant obedience. The sooner we learn this basic but critical principle, the greater fulfillment we will know.

2. The Devil Is a Great Schemer, but He's Out of New Ideas.

Remember, the Devil has no new ideas. Learn his ways once and you know all he has to offer. First John 2:15-16 says, "Because everything that belongs to the world—the lust of the flesh, the lust of the eyes, and the pride in one's lifestyle—is not from the Father, but is from the world." The world has only three things to offer, and the tree in the middle of the Garden held fruit that offered all three:

- It was "good for food"—the lust of the flesh
- It was "pleasing to the eye"—the lust of the eyes
- It was "desirable for gaining wisdom"—the pride in one's lifestyle

The original sin was pride, independent action from God. When Satan came to Eve, he said, in effect, "God is a liar. His Word is not true. Eat the fruit, and you won't die." And listen to these very important words: "God knows that when you eat . . . you will be like God"—and that is an appeal to pride.

Did you ever play "King of the Hill" when you were growing up? The object is to capture the hill and control it. Control is one of our favorite words. The need to control may be stronger for some than others, but trace most of the conflicts in life and you will find the issue is control, from battles in Congress to the Temple Mount. While Satan never had an original thought, he knows our weaknesses and keeps attacking us where we are most vulnerable. Being the King of the Hill makes us feel good. And some are willing to do whatever it takes to maintain the position, even to the selling of their soul.

To be a god yourself, to put yourself on the throne, is the essence of sin, and it is still at the core of all sin. Honor yourself, exalt yourself, bless yourself, take what you want, grasp all you see, look out for Number One, me, I, my, mine. Those are the great words of sin, and they have not changed, nor shall they.

Satan is a crafty and subtle foe, but in many ways our wily enemy is not very bright at all. In thousands of years, he has never come up with a new idea. All sin enters the same way. The lust of the eye, see all you want and want all you see; the lust of the flesh, satisfy me and myself alone; the pride in one's lifestyle, exalt me, worship me, honor me. Guard closely your heart. Set a keeper at the entrance and you will be victorious over sin. Satan is intelligent, wise, and powerful, but he's been out of ideas for centuries and hasn't had a new one since the Garden of Eden.

3. You Can't Beat the System, so Don't Even Try!

Recent verdicts in high profile court cases, such as the O. J. Simpson murder trial, have caused our legal system to come under great scrutiny and serious suspicion. Justice is quite often based on what one can afford. Courts and prison are overcrowded, so deals are cut every day, all in an attempt to keep the system from breaking down. Such is not the case with God's system.

God's laws are immutable. The law of cause and effect is basic to life and spans every area of life. God said, "For when you eat of it you will surely die." They did—and they did. Before sin, man would have physically and spiritually lived forever. But you cannot break the laws of God. You may only break yourself *upon* those laws. Deep in the soul of every sinner is the subtle hiss of the serpent, "But I'm different. I'm the exception. I can get away with it. I won't get caught." But God makes no exceptions, has no pets, plays no favorites, strikes no bargains, and makes no deals. You cannot win at the game of sin.

Someone asked the first American astronaut what he was counting on the most as he lifted into outer space. "It is," he replied, "that when we get up there, God won't change the rules." Those astronauts had studied and trained under prescribed laws of physics and astronomy created and established by almighty God. They staked their lives on those laws and principles, which did not and will not change.

As surely as two plus two will always equal four and night always follows day, what God says, He will do. "The wages of sin is death" (Rom. 6:23 KJV). His laws are immutable. But thank God there is always grace! Immediately upon Adam and Eve's sin, God shed the blood of an innocent animal to cover their shame. It is still by the blood shed on an old rugged cross that He sees us justified before Him.

Judgment day will come for all creation. On that day every knee will bow and every tongue confess that Jesus Christ is Lord. The great news is that we do not have to wait for judgment day to make that confession. God established the plan, and He communicated clearly His expectations for us all. When we accept His Son Jesus Christ as our Savior, we are committing to the system He established at creation. The expectations have never changed; He desires obedience. Don't wait, bow your knee and confess Jesus as Lord today.

CHAPTER 8

Noah

Genesis 6:1–3

1. To Do as You Please Is to Ensure the Loss of Pleasure.

Have you ever had anyone say to you, "Just do as you please"? Those words never came from God; in fact, His explicit command is for us to live a life conforming to the image of His Son Jesus. Only six chapters after the Old Testament begins we read of a people that simply did as they pleased with a complete disregard for the government of God over their lives. Genesis 6:2 says they "married any of them *they chose."* There was complete disregard for God in their choices; the only standard was their own pleasure. They simply did as they pleased, and in so doing were swept from the face of the earth and its selfish pleasures.

It appears in Isaiah that in eternity past, the angels were willing to do God's will. But the first time Lucifer set "I will" above "God's will," sin began. Satan's approach to Eve was "You shall be as gods. God is your enemy. He is withholding from your good. Disregard God. Please yourself. Be a god yourself." Satan's argument is always the same. But to seek her own pleasure was to ensure the loss of the pleasure she had already found. Freedom was in her grasp, but death crouched at the door. As with Eve, so with the angels of God, and so with us.

We are a society of pleasure seekers, working longer hours to make more money so we can embark on greater adventures, craving a fulfillment that can never be found, no matter how scenic or how spectacular the latest and greatest vacation spot may be. But pleasure is at once addictive and insatiable. Read the stories of the people who have the resources to experience all the pleasure that money can buy. Are these the happiest people in the world? Certainly not! The thirst for pleasure can never be satiated by more pleasure.

Leave a child alone with a candy bowl and no adult supervision, and ultimately you will have a child with a very upset stomach. Left alone to do as they please, children do exactly that, and there is a severe price to be paid. Fast food restaurant employees are trained to ask customers if they want to "supersize" their meal. Psychologists tell us the pleasure part of our brain often answers for us in these situations. Bigger must be better, so before we know it, we've cast a vote for what we think will be more pleasure. Unfortunately, more pleasure generally leads to lots of pain. The question should never be, "What do I want to do with my life?" Instead, it should be "What does God want to do in and through my life? How can I fit in to His plan?"

By all accounts, one of the most fulfilled lives in recent years was that of Mother Teresa. Her life was not about pleasure, and in fact, quite often it was about pain. But as she discovered God's plan for her life, she found a passion that led her not to do as she pleased but as He pleased. And she therein found her only true pleasure.

2. The Days of the Rebel Are Numbered, but the Days of the Righteous Are Without End.

Immediately upon the statement that the sons of God took wives from the daughters of men who they chose, God said "My Spirit will not contend with man forever, for he is mortal; his days will be a hundred and twenty years." Hebrews says he limits a certain day. To Belshazzar God said, "You have been weighed on the scales and found wanting. Your kingdom is divided and given to the Medes and Persians" (Dan. 5:27–28). To King Saul God said, in effect, "Your kingdom is over and is given to a man after my own heart."

United States Post Offices had millennium clocks posted behind the counter during 1999. Standing in line watching the time count down toward the year 2000 was both an entertaining and enlightening experience. It did not take long to be reminded that every moment of every day counts. Our minutes are numbered and only God knows when our time is up.

Cemeteries open thousands of graves every day. Scripture records and life confirms our very real mortality. Modern medicine may extend life, but eventually this earthly life is over, and none can stop God's appointed time for our mortal lives to end. *Eternal* life begins the moment we trust Christ as our Savior. Pastors spend uncounted hours with funeral directors. Surprisingly, many in the funeral industry who deal with death on a daily basis have no plans for eternal life for themselves. Mortality is something of which they are very aware, but the rebellious life is more attractive than the righteous life. Billy Graham once said, "The Christian life is the happier life, the holier life, and the harder life." He is so very right.

3. God Doesn't Close the Door on Man Until Man Closes the Door on God.

Our family enjoys using coupons from time to time. "Buy one, get one free" or "twenty percent off" at your favorite restaurant" can be an attractive incentive. Coupons, however normally have stipulations and restrictions about buying a particular meal in order to get another meal for half price or even free. Almost always there is an expiration date in the small print. To qualify for the discount, the coupon must be used prior to the date or it is no longer valid. Some would argue that coupons are only a gimmick to attract us to eat out on a night when we might not normally do so, or to patronize a new restaurant. But nothing about God's grace is a gimmick. His offer is free, and the expiration date is never in small print. Our expiration date is the moment we breathe our last breath in this earthly life. Then, and only then, does His offer of eternal life become null and void.

The song "Amazing Grace" flows off the lips and out of the heart of so many with very little thought. Yet His grace is the most amazing gift ever offered. God has always been a God of grace. Jesus came to this earth full of "grace and truth." In the days of Noah, God offered 120 years of grace, keeping the door of invitation and opportunity open for a very long time. But God's invitation and welcome into the ark was through when the person was through. Genesis 6:5 says, "Every inclination of the thoughts of his heart was only evil all the time." They thought of nothing but evil and did it all the time. As long as there is a spark of interest in one's heart, God will extend His grace. But when a person is through, God is through.

Everyone loves to find good deals. When we buy that car at the right price or catch that special once-a-year clothing sale, our first response is to want everyone to know. But what better deal has ever been offered than the extension of God's grace? The Bible says He is patient with us, not wanting anyone to perish. Everyone has heard the expression "You can't take it with you." Never is that more true than with His offer of eternal life. What are you waiting for? Accept His gift of forgiveness today while the door is still open, and then do some others the greatest favor of their life. Tell them about it!

CHAPTER 9

Abraham

Genesis 12:1–9

1. Clear Direction Requires Immediate Action.

Moving is one of the great headaches of life. No matter how exciting the destination, the hundreds of details—from packing boxes to change of address forms—add up to cause stress. Today's technology allows us to research our new place of residence and make a variety of arrangements before the moving van ever pulls up in our driveway. Imagine, though, what it would be like to be going, but not knowing. That's exactly what God called Abraham to do. In chapter 12:1–3, God tells Abraham, "Leave your country." No specific direction is given or destination identified. Only the blessing and promise of God ensure the heart of the great patriarch. One thing is clear: God said, "Leave." The first three words of verse 4 indicate Abraham's instantaneous response. Without hesitation or question, and certainly lacking any information about either the journey, the provision, or the destination, verse 4 says, "So Abram left."

Joshua 1:1–9 records the call of Joshua and the direction of God to go. Verse 10 says Joshua acted immediately—he ordered the people to get ready, because in three days they would leave. How pleased is our Lord to bless the man or woman whose sensitive heart responds instantly, willingly, and fully, "Yes Lord, I will go right now." The country song asks, "What part of 'no' don't you understand?" The Lord

34

may well ask the believer, "What part of 'go' don't you understand?"

Abraham was a man of obedience and a man of faith. By faith, he responded immediately to the call of God on his life. You wouldn't believe the number of pastors who have asked me to recommend them to another church—as long as it's in Texas. How about you? Are you ready, willing, and able to respond immediately to the call of God on your life? Someone once said, "Faith allows us to step into the future without understanding the present." Walking with God is a life full of surprises, but be assured of this: He walks beside you every step of the way. Today would be a great day to speak the words of the prophet Isaiah, "Here am I Lord, send me!"

2. Great Blessing Demands Great Gratitude.

Thanksgiving always leads to thanks-living! What better way to live than with the knowledge we are all debtors to God for this abundant life He has provided! If you have spent any time around a truly thankful person, you know it is contagious. I once played golf with an older gentleman who thanked the young lady working behind the snack bar for showing up at work that day so we could enjoy some refreshment. She seemed shocked that he would offer his appreciation, and I found myself surprised at his words. I discovered something, though, as I spent more time with him. He was beyond polite; he was truly thankful, and his spirit was infectious. My friend impacted everyone who came his way. I'm convinced that thankful people are happy people, because their priorities are in order and they recognize this principle in their life.

Abraham was such a man, and his life was a reflection of his gratitude to God. In verse 7, God said, "'To your offspring I will give this land.' *So he built an altar there to the* LORD." God expects and deserves immediate acknowledgment for His goodness. Why is it necessary to have national days of thanksgiving? Perhaps because the blessings of God are so numerous they are unrecognized. Impoverished people all over the world would consider the average meal of an American a once-in-a-lifetime celebration feast. Can we be less than constantly grateful? Certainly in those times of special goodness, our Lord deserves our instant and heartfelt expressions of appreciation.

We recently learned that the unborn twins within the womb of our precious daughter-in-law were competing for nourishment and oxygen and the larger was stealing nutrients from the other. The smaller baby would probably die. For nearly two weeks we cried, wept, and begged God for a miracle. On the very next checkup, the doctor said the tiny baby had completely turned in the womb and was growing at a normal rate. To us, it was as if God had placed His hand inside the womb and miraculously and physically turned the baby 180 degrees. Within one second, our eyes filled with tears of gratitude. Within two, we were on our knees giving Him unrestrained thanks and praise.

The apostle Paul encouraged us to give thanks in everything. Test this admonition today. Sit down and make a list of the many things for which you have to be thankful. Don't let circumstances prevent you from seeing the good all around you. Count your blessings today and look for even more tomorrow. You might be amazed at how the clouds will lift and how clearly you see God's hand at work in your life.

3. You Are Never Too Old to Start Again.

My favorite people are those who grow older biologically, but never stop growing spiritually. A number of years ago, I sought the counsel of a veteran pastor whom I had admired from a distance. We stood in the sanctuary of his church and talked about the flow of the worship services. In the midst of our conversation, he said, "Let me tell you about something new I tried last Sunday." I was amazed. Here was a man who had pastored for over fifty years and was still trying new things! What a wonderful lesson I learned about continuing to grow, and what an inspiration he was to me!

God created us for growth, and His Word is filled with example after example of men and women He used to do a new thing even in their later years. Abraham and Sarah provide two of the best. Genesis 12:4 says Abraham was seventy-five years of age. Today at that age most persons are making plans to die. But He who has a wonderful blueprint for our lives was making plans for Abraham to live. Living with optimism and anticipation is the zest of life. I think of my dear friends Marge and Chuck Caldwell, who in their mid-eighties live every day as if it were the first day of the rest of their lives. My wife's parents sold their mobile home, packed themselves, and moved to Houston at age eighty-seven to begin life again. In Christ we don't have to age, and the best is always yet to come.

Several years ago, a study was made of several persons in their nineties. They responded to this question: "If you had life to live over again, what would you do differently?" The top three responses were these: take more risks, spend more time in reflection, and do more that would live on after they were gone. That's great advice, regardless of your age. Eliminate the risk by partnering with God. Spend some time in prayer and meditation, and allow the Holy Spirit to speak to your heart during those moments of reflection. Invest yourself in the lives of those around you, and the dividends will be eternal. You can be like Abraham—eternally young and never too old to start anew.

CHAPTER 10

Sarah

Genesis 12:10–13

1. Minor Mistakes Can Have Major Consequences.

Several years ago a major power plant in the northwestern part of our country was completely shut down. The loss of electricity and cost of repairs were enormous. After an extensive search, engineers determined the cause of the outage: a five-cent washer! The plant crew spent millions of dollars and hundreds of man-hours, all because of a tiny misplaced metal part. Small mistakes can have huge consequences.

How many times have you heard people say, "Oh, if I could just go back and make a different choice!" Sarah experienced the dangerous results of choosing not to follow God's commands completely. To be clear, Sarah was apparently innocent, however, of any wrong. A simple pawn in the game of life, she would suffer greatly because of a well-intended, yet serious mistake her husband made.

When the news came of an impending famine, Abraham's first thought was to run. That little sojourn down into Egypt would be a fiasco of monumental proportions. God had told them to leave Haran and go into Canaan, to which they responded with instant obedience. But God gave no command for Abraham to take his family from Canaan into Egypt. Abraham could have saved himself from great heartache if he had simply followed the Lord's direction completely.

The story of Abraham is filled with references to "the LORD said" and "the Lord told Abraham." Why this time did he act alone? Perhaps he thought the move was an insignificant and obvious decision he could make without consulting God. But a step without God's leadership is always a step down. Samson went *down* to Timnath; David looked *down* from his rooftop; Jonah went *down* to Tarsus. They were seemingly innocent and insignificant mistakes, but even the slightest step away from God's leadership and out of God's will is a step downward. Abraham and Sarah should never have agreed to go down to Egypt at all.

2. Downward Spirals Always Increase in Velocity.

Wrong decisions usually lead to more wrong decisions, creating even greater wrong. Like a tornado whose winds blow the most fiercely at the end of the funnel, we do not commit more sin without digging a deeper hole and heaping the dirt on top of ourselves. On the surface Abraham's move to Egypt was the obvious one to make. Perhaps he thought, *Do I have to pray about everything? Surely this is an easy and natural decision.* But choosing to rely on human reason led to a lie about Sarah, essentially selling her into adultery with the Egyptian Pharaoh. Genesis 12:15 says, "She was taken into his palace." In verse 19, Pharaoh admits, "I took her to be my wife." What do you think that means? At the very least, Abraham's foolishness sold her into slavery to Pharaoh's family, if not into his harem as a concubine. The rebuke of Pharaoh in 12:18–19 is stinging. Nothing is ever quite as devastating as when the unrighteous rebuke the righteous for their unrighteousness. For Abraham it was a serious blow because of a careless and thoughtless choice that did not include God.

Do you pride yourself on having good common sense? How many times have you heard someone say, "I made a decision based on the best information available." Maybe you've said that at some point in your life. Let me ask you a question. Did the best information available include time spent alone with God, searching to hear His voice, seeking His perfect will for your life? If not, then you certainly did not have the best information available. God stands ready to hear our cries for help. Better to cry to Him for guidance *before* the fact than for deliverance *after.*

Some folks have a hard time asking for directions. These same people generally brag about their great sense of direction. But if I'm heading down a wrong road, driving farther and going faster do nothing to help me get where I am going. In fact, it delays my arrival at my intended destination, and all because I was too proud or too impatient to simply ask for directions. The consequences of failing to follow God in complete obedience are enormous. Ask around. There are plenty of people who will tell you that downward spirals always increase in velocity.

3. Selfishness Is Its Own Reward.

In the days of manual typewriters, one key always wore out the fastest. It was the letter "I." According to the people who repair typewriters, it was not because of the number of times the key was punched, but because of the force with which the key was struck. Selfishness comes rather naturally for us. We evaluate and make our decisions based on how the situation impacts us personally, quite often with very little thought for others involved.

Abraham demonstrated world-class selfishness when he made the decision to pass Sarah off as his sister. This entire bizarre incident was the selfish fault of Abraham. Verse 13 says, "Say you are my sister, so that I will be treated well for your sake." Abraham wasn't thinking about his wife; he was thinking about Abraham. An innocent and faithful woman was thrust into the arms of another man by a husband whose only motivation was his selfish intent to save himself. But before we are too quick to judge Abraham, we need to take a look in the mirror. How many times have we said yes to an assignment or a promotion without any thought about how it might affect our family? And have we ever told a half-truth in order to protect our image? We most often learn humility by being humiliated! Selfishness is a guaranteed recipe to cook up a big batch of humiliation.

CHAPTER II

Isaac

Genesis 26:1–7

1. God Knows Us Better Than We Know Ourselves.

Where do you go when times get tough? Quite often we revert to our weaknesses. Often when we are depressed, we eat more or sleep more. Others may go shopping and run up large credit card bills. Hard times can turn us toward God, or they can take us to a place where we can feed our loneliness. Isaac faced some hard times in his life, and one took him in the wrong direction.

When there was a great famine in the land, Isaac went to King Abimelech of the Philistines in the land of Gerar. God knew Isaac so well, just as He does us, that He intervened in his plans. Why? Because He clearly knew that the spiritual DNA of Isaac's father, Abraham, was pressed deeply into Isaac's genes. Gerar is in the southwest part of Israel on the way to Egypt. God knew that, like Isaac, Jacob was headed straight for Egypt. He who knows the thoughts and intentions of our hearts, who created us in the body of our mothers, who knit us together in the womb, knows our thoughts before we think them. He knows us better than we know ourselves. How foolish we are in not seeking His wisdom and direction at every juncture of our life!

I remember a time in my own life when I was seeking God's direction about a very important decision I needed to make. In the midst of the pressure of trying to make the right choice, my wife encouraged me to seek the counsel of a friend

41

we both trusted and respected. I resisted her suggestion because I thought this friend would not tell me what I wanted to hear. Have you been there? Out of the blue, this friend called the house to talk about another matter. Near the end of the conversation I shared some of the turmoil I was experiencing as I sought God's direction about an important life decision. God used his words to give me assurance about the decision I was to make. God not only knew exactly what was going on in my life, He also cared enough to direct one of His servants to speak the words I had been thinking but had not been able to express.

2. We Benefit Much from the Righteousness of Others.

As a teenager, I spent quite a bit of time at a best friend's house. His father was a carpenter, a giant of a man, a man of few words and much love for the Lord. One of my most vivid memories is walking down the hallway in their modest home and seeing this big man on his knees. He was dressed for work in overalls, leather boots, and a blue shirt and was kneeling beside his bed, talking to his Heavenly Father about the day ahead and about me. My friend's dad has gone on to be with his Savior, and though I did not realize it at the time, today I am still reaping the benefits of his righteousness. His example is firmly planted in the theater of my mind.

Isaac benefited from the righteousness of his father. In verse 5 God reiterated and even expanded the promise of Abraham to Isaac. Stay in this land, He said, "And I will bless you *because Abraham obeyed me* and kept my requirements." The Bible says He did it for one reason and one reason alone: for Abraham's sake. Study Scripture and you will find many examples of people, even nonbelievers, reaping the blessings because godly men and women obeyed God. Genesis 39:5 says, "The LORD blessed the household of the Egyptian *because of Joseph.*"

I am married to the most wonderful Christian woman in the world. She prays and reads God's Word with a passion and truly loves her Lord, I believe, far more than does her husband. Through the years I have lived with a constant awareness that blessings often accrue to my benefit which our Lord showers upon this His loving daughter. Spend the time to take a spiritual inventory of your life. Are you enjoying the benefits of some righteous individual? If so, give thanks for that person and for the powerful testimony of your friend's righteous life. Now two harder questions. Who might be watching you? Whose life is benefitting from your righteousness?

3. Only the Cross Can Break the Curse.

Abraham's sin kept repeating itself in the life of his son, Isaac. Isaac started down the very road to Egypt which once his father had trod. He would sacrifice the integrity of Rebecca, as did Abraham with Sarah. He lied, just as his father had, and said his wife was his sister. He, too, was rebuked by an unbeliever (Gen. 26:10). The sins of the fathers, indeed, tend to recur in the lives of their children. This does not mean we *pay* for the sins of our parents, rather, that we are *affected* by their sins. Unfortunately, many believers simply do not understand that the cycle of that sin was broken at the Cross. We need not go through endless genealogies trying to determine and break ancestral curses. Hear the mighty words of Paul in Galatians 3:13, "Christ has redeemed us from the curse of the law by becoming a curse for us, because it is written: 'Cursed is everyone who is hung on a tree.'" No provision was made for the Old Testament believer like that which is made for the New Testament Christian at Calvary.

Maybe instead of asking, What would Jesus do? we need to be reminded exactly what Jesus did! His death on the cross was the final payment for the bondage of sin. It was the emancipation proclamation for all who would accept His invitation to receive forgiveness for sin and enter into a life of righteousness. If you have ever paid off a note at the bank, you have received papers that give you cause for celebration. Stamped across the note are the words "Paid in Full." The debt has been canceled, the obligation has been met, nothing is left to be paid. No one was celebrating around the cross on the day Jesus was crucified. Some were gambling, some weeping, others simply staring in disbelief. But from our vantage point—beyond Calvary—we can celebrate!! Death has no more sting, and death will never win the victory. The curse is over, for the Cross provided the bridge to lead us home!

CHAPTER 12

Jacob

Genesis 33:1–4

1. We Fear from Others What We Despise in Ourselves.

How much time do you spend in front of a mirror? Have you ever noticed some mirrors are more forgiving than others? A well-lighted mirror can reveal the physical flaws and imperfections on a face but do nothing to reveal what is hidden in a heart. Perhaps that is why God sends people into our lives—to provide a living mirror that reveals what is taking place in our hearts.

Think about some of the people in your life. Now think about what you fear most from them. Strange how that works. We may hate the fact that we lie about others, all the while wondering if they are lying about us. While the gossip hates his own sin, his greater pain often comes from the fear that everyone is gossiping about him.

Jacob was a deceiver. His deceitfulness began early in life and formed a pattern that followed him all of his days. Quite often, while he was busy deceiving, he was also being deceived. Jacob had stolen his father's birthright, and the day of reckoning had come. The long awaited and much dreaded meeting with Esau was at hand. Always the schemer, Jacob had a plan. He would send gifts ahead to attempt to win the favor of Esau, hoping to soften the memory of his previous deception. His maidservants and their children would lead the way. Leah and her children would bring up the rear, and Rachel and Joseph would be in the middle. Did he imagine they would protect him? Did he suppose Esau would not kill him for their sake? The root of his fear was himself—he knew that, if the roles had been reversed, he would have taken revenge.

To Jacob's surprise, God had worked in Esau's heart, and Jacob's twin brother was neither spiteful, conniving, nor revengeful. He was simply a man touched by God. Esau was a spiritual mirror in Jacob's life. No more blessed words occur in Scripture than those in verse 4: "Esau ran to meet Jacob and embraced him; he threw his arms around his neck and kissed him." What if the roles had been reversed? Jacob knew what he would have done, and that's what made him so afraid. We do, indeed, fear from others that which we most despise in ourselves.

2. God Always Meets You More than Halfway.

When we truly meet God, He surprises us with joy. Imagine the wonder in the soul of Jacob as Esau ran to him and embraced him! Scripture is full of stories of God meeting His loved ones more than halfway. The prodigal returned home, rehearsing a speech he never had to give. Jesus said that while the son was still *a long way off,* the father ran to him, and before he knew what was happening, a party was being planned in his honor. The prodigal got neither what he expected nor what he deserved.

Have you ever made arrangements to meet someone halfway? Halfway seems fair to us, the right thing to do. But none of us are able to meet God halfway, and the good news is we don't have to. A relationship with God is not a fifty-fifty partnership, and we don't have to play, "Let's Make a Deal." We simply accept His gift of salvation and His promise to never leave us or forsake us. Grace leads us all the way home.

3. You Can't Earn the Love of One Who Truly Loves You.

Love is a many-splendored thing, and I think a many splintered thing. Love can be extremely frustrating until we learn that you cannot make someone love you, and if they do, you cannot keep them from loving you. In verse 8 Esau asks, "What do you mean by all these droves I met?" And Jacob answered, "To find favor in your eyes, my Lord." Jacob lived by the adage, "You scratch my back, and I'll scratch yours." He was convinced he could buy anything he wanted, including his brother's mercy.

Esau did not require Jacob to shower lavish gifts upon him as a condition of his love. Aren't we like Jacob at times? We try to win God's love by bringing monetary or other gifts to Him, but God's gift of His grace is based on His love, and on His very nature. Quit trying to perform to earn God's grace. He already loves you more than you can know.

God's grace goes against almost everything we know about how our culture works. Consequently, we can get caught up in our own performance and try to build a resumé with God. Instead of serving God out of love and affection, we try to prove something He never asks us to prove. When was the last time you simply rested in God's presence and reveled in His love?

CHAPTER 13

Joseph

Genesis 39:7–12

1. Trust Is the Greatest Motivation to Purity.

Madison Avenue and Hollywood are convinced that with simply a little temptation we can be convinced. Virtually every advertisement and television show is filled with the sensual and the sexual. But temptation is not new; it has been around since the Garden of Eden. God trusted us enough to give us the freedom to choose and the opportunity to completely trust Him when we find ourselves face-to-face with temptation.

Probably no one faced as powerful a sexual temptation as did the young and virile Joseph. The temptation of Potiphar's wife was powerful and real, her invitation to him open and unabashed: "Come to bed with me." Joseph's first defense was to consider the trust placed in him by Potiphar. Genesis 39:8 says, "My master does not concern himself with anything in the house; everything he owns he has entrusted to my care." In other words, "Your husband trusts me so much he doesn't even keep records. How can I do such a thing? How could I break such a sacred trust by being untrustworthy with you?" Often it is said that the doctrine of eternal security is license to sin. I say it is motivation *not* to sin. The fact that my wife trusts me out of town and out of sight for days at a time does not encourage me to sin; rather, it encourages me to the highest level of faithfulness to the one who trusts me, and whom I would not disappoint for anything.

48

2. A Big Picture Perspective Guarantees Good Short-Range Decisions.

How many times have you heard someone say, "I just wasn't thinking," or "I acted on impulse," as they suffer the consequences. Many times in counseling I have tried to suggest to a young person to look a long way down the road to gain a broader perspective. But ours is a "here and now" culture with a "seize the moment" attitude, especially when it comes to pleasure.

In verse 9 Joseph says, "How then could I do such a wicked thing and sin against God?" More important than his sin against himself, Potiphar's wife, or her husband would be Joseph's sin against God. The short view meant great pleasure. The long view, great wickedness. The human view saw a great opportunity. The divine view saw a great offense.

The book of Hebrews tells us that, like Joseph, Jesus chose to endure pain rather than enjoy the pleasures of the world for a season. Story after story in Scripture reveals the importance of expanding our horizons and seeking first the kingdom of God, rather than chasing what so appeals at the moment. You've seen the bumper sticker that says, "Life is uncertain, eat dessert first!" Satan would like nothing better than for us to buy into that attitude. Pursue that mentality and we all become hedonists, seeking after the things of the flesh. What if Joseph had succumbed to temptation rationalizing that "no one will know" or "just this once." His life and the lives of millions would have been different. He proved to God that he could be trusted on that day, and God honored him in the days to come. The long look is always the best look.

3. Persecution for Righteousness Ultimately Brings Blessing.

Jesus made this principle clear in the Beatitudes, those verses in Matthew that introduce the Sermon on the Mount—the preamble of the "Constitution of the Kingdom." Few of us would sign up for a heavy dose of persecution, yet many feel that nothing would be as helpful for the Christian church today. The furnace of affliction, while not something we would seek, forges our character like nothing else. No wonder James wrote the words, "Consider it a great joy . . . whenever you experience various trials . . ." Many of us could testify to the sustaining grace of God and the powerful development of our maturity after we endured persecution for the sake of the kingdom.

Joseph could offer that testimony, for he suffered temptation, scorn, false accusations, humiliation, and imprisonment because of his stand for holiness and righteousness. And was he blessed? Indeed, he was. He became the second most powerful person in the Egyptian Empire. In persecution for righteousness or in ridicule from others for the sake of Christ, there is great reward. One of my favorite pastors says, "When given enough time, God can always make something good happen." When it comes to persecution for righteousness' sake, that's a promise. God will reward those who stand for Him.

4. Time Spent Fighting God's Battles Is Never Wasted Time.

The poet James Dickey wrote a book titled *Deliverance*. It is the story of four suburbanites who take a canoe trip down a wild white-water river in North Georgia. On the way, two are ambushed and one sexually assaulted by murderous locals. They make a hair-raising escape, and the rest of the story is about their hazardous trip down the canyon, with one of the locals stalking and shooting at them from above. When they finally reach safety, they can't even talk about their ordeal. They are delivered—barely—but their minds are scarred for life. James Dickey's book is, on one level, a modern morality play. Life itself is like the passage down a wild, primitive canyon, where we are easy marks as temptation threatens at every turn. Like these men when they began their outing, we often manage to laugh and sing and pretend we are having fun. But the evil one is always there, lying in wait, ready to spring, and anxious to devour us.

But we need to remember, long hours of struggle with temptation make us strong. Like a mud wall increasingly fortified with every incoming cannon ball, the character of the believer grows during times of temptation. Temptation builds character. The little song we used to sing in Sunday school said it well:

*"Yield not to temptation, for yielding is sin.
Each vict'ry will help you some other to win."*

Succumbing to temptation destroys us. Successfully resisting it builds us. Remember, temptation is not sin. Temptation is the invitation to sin. It is not evil. It is the opportunity to do evil. And our Lord allows it in our lives to make us strong.

CHAPTER 14

Moses

Exodus 3:1–6, 10–11, 14

1. The Greatest Revelation of God Can Begin at the End of Your Road.

The burning bush experience did not happen at the front side of the desert near the palaces of Egypt, but at the back, near the tents of Midian. The prodigal came to himself in the pit. Samson gave his life in the Philistine court. Jonah found God, as he had never known Him, tangled in seaweed at the bottom of the ocean. The three Hebrew children met the son of God when they met the fourth man in the fire. The dying thief's last words were, "Lord, remember me when you come into your kingdom." Jesus' first words to him were, "This day shall thou be with me in paradise." When you come to the end of your rope, tie a knot and hang on with one hand. When you extend the other, you will find the hand of Jesus.

Marathon runners know something about pressing on when they feel like quitting. In the Boston Marathon is a legendary obstacle. Starting at mile thirteen of the course a runner must make it up a number of hills. At mile nineteen the exhausted runner encounters Heartbreak Hill, the longest, steepest hill in the race. What makes this hill even worse is that world-class runners "hit the wall" around mile eighteen or nineteen. Their bodies have become depleted of glycogen stored in the muscles, have replaced it with lactic acid, and are screaming for oxygen. When you hit the wall, you feel like you're going to die. Heartbreak Hill tests runners to the very core of their determination and their strength.

There are Heartbreak Hills in life. Life is not on a level grade. We have problems, and then we have bigger problems. And at times we face Heartbreak Hill. Those are the moments when we really meet God and find Him sufficient to meet every need of life.

2. Friendship with God Doesn't Mean Familiarity with God.

My favorite role in life is being a dad. Some of the happiest moments of my life have been experienced in that relationship between father and child. But I've discovered the only way that our relationship really works is to remember who is the father and who is the child. Fatherhood means that my responsibilities go much further than simply that of being a friend. There are moments when I must provide leadership, assert authority, and sometimes offer unwanted discipline.

The best friendships are filled with respect. Friendship with God is no exception. In Exodus 3:4 God called to Moses out of the burning bush. In verse 5 He said, "Do not come any closer." Further, "Take off your sandals, for the place where you are standing is holy ground." God said to Moses, "Come this far, but no farther." God's love for us and friendship with us must not allow us to presume upon His holiness and sovereignty.

Most of us know people who talk about God as, "the old man in the sky" or "the man upstairs." Such persons have very little concept of our Heavenly Father. Their familiarity embodies no respect and absolutely no understanding of the God of the ages. While it is true that He is a friend who sticks closer than a brother, it is also true that we dare not presume on God. Removing our shoes is always in order when we stand on holy ground.

3. Success Doesn't Depend on Who I Am, but upon Who God Is.

When we believe we are the King of the Hill, we believe we determine our own destiny and govern our own lives, creating a world where all of life revolves around Me and Mine. In verse 11 Moses asked, "Who am I to do such an impossible task?" In verse 14 God replies, "The issue is not who you are, but who I am." God is the real King of the Hill, but as long as we attempt to occupy His rightful spot, we will be afraid like Moses. Our focus will invariably be our own inadequacies. But when we see God in all His majesty, we are convinced that no task is too great for Him. Consider the challenge you are facing today, then ask the question: "Is this too much for God to handle?" Change in our perspectives can bring great change in our circumstances.

Jesus said, "Without me you can do nothing." Think of it: nothing—*no thing*—a thing that does not exist. That's what we are. That's what we can do without Him. Remember, He didn't say, "We can't do much." He said we can do nothing.

CHAPTER 15

Pharaoh

Exodus 4:15–16; 12:12–13; 14:9

1. No One Can Do for Us What God Would Do through Us.

Moses argued that he could not speak for the Lord because he stuttered, and Exodus 4:14–16 records God's response: "Then the LORD's anger burned against Moses and he said, 'What about your brother, Aaron the Levite? I know he can speak well. He is already on his way to meet you, and his heart will be glad when he sees you. You shall speak to him and put words in his mouth; I will help both of you speak and will teach you what to do. He will speak to the people for you, and it will be as if he were your mouth and as if you were God to him.'" Aaron could speak to the people for Moses—that was relatively easy. But God said that Moses had to do the really hard job, standing before the Pharaoh, by himself.

Someone listening to Moses make excuses before God about all the reasons he could not approach the Pharaoh might have wondered why the Lord would choose such a man. After all, if his brother Aaron was going to do all the talking, why not simply skip the middle man and make Aaron the leader of the Exodus? One need only fast forward the story to know that God knew exactly what He was doing when He called to Moses out of the burning bush on the back side of a desert. We see some of yesterday, a little of today, and none of tomorrow, but God sees it all. As Moses climbed to the top of the mountain to meet with God, Aaron led the people to worship a golden calf.

Upon his return, Moses, refined by the Lord, is no longer the insecure man God had chosen to lead His people. Was Moses the right man for the job of leading over a million people on the world's largest backpacking trip? Absolutely! When God wants to teach us dependence on Him, He always takes us to the desert. It happened with Moses as God prepared him for this unbelievable assignment and used the desert to work in the lives of the Israelites. Next time you find yourself enduring a desert experience, stop and consider what God may be wanting to do in and through you.

We live in a day of great specialization, even in ministry. Churches and ministries are employing a host of specialists to assist in kingdom work. As a pastor I have learned through the years that someone can help me visit the hospitals, counsel, administer, and even assist in sermon research. But no one else can preach for me or make the hard decisions every pastor must make. That is no accident. God intends it that way, for the things God would do through us, no one else can do *for* us.

2. Timing Is Everything with God.

Consider some of the expressions we use about time: in the nick of time, just in time, on time, killing time, half-time, bed time, nap time, dinner time, and the list goes on. But consider how important it is to understand and live in God's time. Moses obviously understood, and Psalm 90:12 expresses his prayer: "Teach us to number our days aright, that we may gain a heart of wisdom."

Plague after plague came upon Egypt, yet God only further hardened the heart of Pharaoh. Note that the text does not say, "Pharaoh hardened his own heart," but rather that God hardened his heart. Why? Because God was not going to let him say yes until *after* the death of the firstborn—the night of the Passover blood. The most significant imagery in the Old Testament is deliverance from satanic bondage by the death of an innocent sacrifice. A shadow of an old rugged cross lay across that night in Egypt, fifteen hundred years before Calvary. That night had to happen. It is the high point of Old Testament literature. Nothing compares to the trail of blood from the Garden of Eden to the Garden of Gethsemane, and because Pharaoh's heart was so hard, it took time to bring him to the high point of Old Testament Scripture. Only a deathblow would break the bondage of God's people.

Did you ever play the children's game, "My Dad's Better than Your Dad?" Kids like to argue about whose dad is the strongest or smartest. Something like that took place as Pharaoh and the Egyptians endured plague after plague. Each plague of Egypt was an attack on an Egyptian deity. The crops, the cattle, and the Nile River, each subjected to a plague, were objects of worship for the Egyptians. God was sending a powerful message that there was only one true God, and that everyone and everything else was a pretender.

But only the death of the firstborn could be the consummate foreshadow of the cross. Only after many other major plagues could God bring Pharaoh to the point at which he gave in, becoming the ultimate Old Testament example of Satan's power broken by innocent blood.

3. Even the Mighty Victory at Calvary Is Just the Beginning for the Believer.

One wonders what Moses and the children of Israel must have thought as they escaped the tyranny of slavery in Egypt. Surely it was too good to be true. After all these years of serving Pharaoh, they were free at last; or were they? Not long after Pharaoh released the Hebrews, he diligently began to pursue them. "Let not one Israelite escape," he commanded his troops. Were they surprised? Probably not, for surely they expected as much from a Pharaoh who had endured ten plagues. Pharaoh did not realize it, but once again God was using him to accomplish His will, as the children of Israel would have another opportunity to see God's awesome power on display in the wilderness.

When we trust Christ as our Savior, we may leave the altar thinking the battle is over, when it is just beginning. In fact, we go forth not to struggle to victory, but by faith to appropriate a victory already won. We go forth not alone, but with the One who promised never to leave us nor forsake us. Will there be obstacles and roadblocks along the journey? Indeed, there will be, but they will only build our spiritual muscle.

In the wilderness struggle, the steel of our faith is tempered. Battles are there to win. Giants are there to overcome. If we never have problems, how will we know that God can solve them? If we don't have needs, how will we learn that God will meet them? Always remember the battle is the Lord's. The journey may be long and the obstacles great, but beginning at the Cross, God assumes responsibility for the journey and guarantees the victory.

CHAPTER 16

Joshua

Joshua 6:3–5, 18–19; 7:1

1. Only Full Obedience Equates to Full Blessing.

The miracle at Jericho was a milestone for Israel. The instructions were clear: seven times around, seven days, priests in front, blow the trumpets and shout. How often they may have been tempted to quit! What would have happened had they only marched six days? Would they have had six-sevenths of a blessing? Not at all. What if only half the people had shouted? Would only half the wall have fallen down? Hardly. Ninety percent of the people marching and shouting would not have brought down ninety percent of the wall.

Faithfulness is virtually synonymous with obedience and there are no degrees of faithfulness. Do you want to be married to a husband or wife who is pretty faithful? The sin of Saul, as well as many like him, was partial obedience. A halfway commitment does not equate to halfway blessing, but to no blessing at all.

2. The Activity of God Is Always Supernatural.

How did the walls fall down? Unbelievers say that vibration caused the collapse, and vibration does have a powerful effect on structure. "Route, step, march, route, step," the army is commanded at the bridge. The constant drumming of feet in unison can weaken a bridge, so the soldiers break the rhythm of the march when they cross it. However, a clever plan of

59

synchronized marching didn't bring down Jericho, but God's plan did. Joshua's obedience to God's instruction teaches us three things:

- Following God's plan takes faith. This was a battle plan never before used in the annals of warfare. To the military-minded, it made no sense. To the doubters, it seemed foolhardy. And not a few Israelites must have thought Joshua had lost his mind!
- Following God's plan takes courage. Did some of the Israelites feel a tad foolish? Surely there were catcalls from the ramparts of Jericho. To show up for six consecutive days, march around the city and go back to camp required a different type of courage from what warfare requires. It took courage to follow God's instructions rather than one's own logic.
- Following God's plan takes persistence. One also recalls Naaman, who dipped seven times in the Jordan (2 Kings 5:9). When the first or second repetition produced nothing, his inclination was to quit. God honors faithful persistence. His lessons are always, "Keep on asking. Keep on seeking. Keep on knocking."

There is no human explanation for the destruction of the walls of Jericho. It was not the vibration of the marchers or the penetration of the shout that crumbled the stones. It was the supernatural power of God in response to the obedience of His children. They did not help God. They didn't start the wall swaying a bit so God could finish the job. Their obedience allowed God to do it, but it did not help God to do it. It is always by His power, always of His might, and always for His glory. We do not accomplish the purposes of God. We only move our lives into line with them, that He may accomplish His mighty will and show His power through us.

3. Minor Mistakes Have Major Consequences.

Almost lost in the impact of the awesome annihilation of Jericho's walls is the account of the plundering of Jericho.

Undoubtedly to Israel, of secondary importance to the wonder they had just seen was what they still wanted. How quickly they turned the focus from what God had done to what they wanted to do. Most important on that day was *their* will. They soon forgot the clear command of God, "Don't take the devoted things." Quickly their attitude became "I'll do it anyway," and the result was their humiliating defeat at Ai.

One man, just one of thousands, hid the forbidden treasure of Jericho beneath the tented secrecy of his own sin. But massive and devastating was the consequence at Ai, and Israel never got over it. After Israel's defeat, their enemies no longer trembled before the name of Israel and her God.

Vast are the implications of Achan's secret sin. But secret sin is to God no secret at all. The anger of the Lord burned against all the children of Israel because of one man's disobedience. The sin of one person always affects much more than just his own life. For Israel, secret sin translated to corporate responsibility. The men of Ai killed about thirty-six men.

Brought up on rugged individualism, Americans often overlook the corporate aspect of sin and responsibility. Paul wrote to the church at Corinth that "if one member suffers, all the members suffer with it" (1 Cor. 12:26). Secret sin confuses God's people. In verse 7:7, Joshua cried out, "Ah, Sovereign LORD, why?" The insidious thing about secret sin is that it brings on God's judgment for no apparent reason. Then, speculation leads to false conclusions, and God's people become discouraged. Achan thought his sin to be minor, but it resulted in major consequences for the people of Israel. Joshua sought God's will and led God's people to repentance and restoration. Leaders like Joshua will not be content with defeat; they will actively engage in understanding God's purpose in order to set things right.

CHAPTER 17

Elijah

1 Kings 17:1; 18:32–35, 38

1. Your Past Is Not Nearly as Important as God's Purpose.

J. Oswald Sanders once wrote of Elijah, "He was like a meteor that flashed across the inky blackness of Israel's spiritual night." Read the story again, and you will discover Elijah appeared on the scene like a superhero coming to the rescue. Yet we know so little about where he came from and how he came to be God's instrument to confront the powerful and wicked King Ahab. Interestingly, the writer of 1 Kings gives only his name and his town of origin. He blows into history like a tornado, without credential or reputation.

He is simply known as "Elijah the Tishbite," who was just one of the many who lived in Gilead.

In spite of an apparent lack of qualifications, God had a distinct purpose for his life. When the young evangelist began his crusades, people might have thought, "Why, this is only Billy Graham from North Carolina," but God had a mighty mission for this man as well. Far too often the longer the pedigree the shorter the dog. I would rather be simply "John Bisagno from Texas" and let God get all the glory from whatever He chooses to accomplish through my life. A call to the ministry is a call to prepare, and the importance of preparation cannot be overstated. But God always has a few models around like Billy Graham, to remind us it's still all about Him.

62

The story of Elijah reminds us we do not need some thrilling testimony from our past in order to be used for His glory. Many of us have a rather ordinary past, but with God we always have an extraordinary future. Don't let an average yesterday cause you to minimize your potential today and tomorrow. Elijah's lackluster past did not prevent him from stepping up to the plate when God called his name. The result was the confrontation at Mount Carmel, possibly the most powerful event in the Old Testament apart from creation and the Red Sea. What does God have in store for you? Will you be ready? Or have you convinced yourself that God could never use ordinary you? Prepare yourself for the future, focus on our resurrected Lord, and be amazed at what He will do with your life.

2. The Harder the Situation, the Better God Likes It.

As residents of big cities, some of us have not seen the majesty displayed nightly in the heavens for a long time. Have you ever noticed that the darker the night, the brighter the light shines, and that light always defeats darkness? I'm convinced that God loves dark places, because in those moments His light and love can shine the brightest. Israel was a dark place in the days of Elijah, but the darkness of the hour was the perfect backdrop against which God could reveal His power.

The confrontation on Mount Carmel was not merely a battle between Elijah and the prophets of Baal; it was an opportunity for God to remind His people one more time that He alone was God, and that they must have no other. It was the spirit of God who impressed on the heart of Elijah to water the sacrifice once and again, and then again. This was no bizarre display of a presumptive prophet, but the way of the God of Israel. He is the same God who parted the Red Sea, declaring, "Stand still and see the salvation of the Lord." He is the same God who impressed upon Gideon that a victory against thirty thousand enemies, wrought at the hand of thirty thousand Israelites, would leave no room for His glory.

God worked a miracle with Gideon's three hundred men, outnumbered ten to one. When your back's against the wall and you face an impossible situation, get ready to see a miracle. When you've come to the end of your rope, go to your knees, get in the Word, and get ready to see the hand of God.

Former President George Bush talked about a "thousand points of light." It was his regular practice to give awards to people and programs that shed the light of mercy in places of dark despair. Jesus called Himself the light of the world, but He took it much further when He told His disciples, "You are the light of the world." If you find yourself living in a dark place, be encouraged, for your light may shine even more brightly, causing more people to see the Lord. If you find yourself in a difficult situation, have no fear, God loves to do the impossible. He did it on Mount Carmel and longs to do it again.

3. The Character of the Hero May Be Forged on the Anvil of the Ordinary.

How would you feel if someone called you a "Tishbite"? If you like to think of yourself as rough and rugged, then you probably would take great pride in being called a Tishbite. Elijah the Tishbite came from a place that would best be described as challenging; and though his presence on the stage of Israel's history was abrupt, there is no reason to believe he suddenly became at Carmel what he was not already at Gilead. The first words out of his mouth to a powerful and wicked king were, "From now on it doesn't rain unless I say so." Heroes are not born in a minute. Courage comes with holiness. The man secure in Christ and His Word is secure in himself. The acts of Moses took place over forty years of internship in the wilderness. You may be sure that God's mighty hand had been forging his backbone of steel long before.

I was having dinner in a home not long ago in which several children sat with us at the table. During the opening moments of the meal, the mother inquired about what kind of day her children had experienced. They all answered the same way: "Regular day." I understood, because quite often my own children have given me the same answer to my inquiries about their day. But I wonder if there are truly any regular days? Is God not using our education, our experience, even our ordinariness, to prepare us for what lies ahead? I'm convinced that God works through ordinary, even unlikely people, and their ordinary days, to accomplish His purpose. Next time you are tempted to describe your day as ordinary, consider whether God might be preparing you for a Mount Carmel experience.

CHAPTER 18

Elisha

2 Kings 4:1–7

1. He Who Seeks God's Will Finds Much More Than He Seeks.

Like Solomon, Elisha received the privilege of asking for an extraordinary gift. If you could have anything, what would it be? Far too many of us would consider our own personal need or desire and would ask for something with short-term benefits. Elisha's request was not for position or wealth, but for power. "Let me inherit a double portion of your spirit," Elisha asked Elijah. Though it was not Elijah's to give, this great prophet and mentor gave his student the promise that it was possible. "If you see me when I am taken from you, it will be yours . . . ." What was Elisha really seeking? Was he trying to be even more successful than Elijah? I don't think so—I believe Elisha wanted even more of God than he had witnessed in Elijah's life, and what he had seen in Elijah was powerful.

The power that filled all the empty pots of a Samaritan widow came from an anointing that meant more to him than life. Could he have known that a double portion of power would translate into saving the two lives of the widow's sons? Probably not! Can we ever know just how God's power is going to be used in our lives? Definitely not! But he who seeks God with all his heart finds much more than he seeks. David reminded us of this in Psalms 37:4 when he wrote, "Delight yourself in the Lord and He will give you the desires of your heart." Our Lord tells us, as recorded in Matthew 6:33, "Seek first the Kingdom of God and His righteousness, and all these things will be provided for you." Seek God with all your heart, soul, mind, and strength, and leave the results to Him.

2. God Meets Us at the Most Common Point of Our Need.

How often in Scripture do we see a God who starts with nothing? The widow was a very poor woman, indeed. She had nothing in the house—no food, no resources, no discretionary funds, nothing with which to barter for the life of her sons. Obviously she had borrowed before. Apparently she had been faithful to return what she borrowed. She was a nice woman, and the neighbors were eager to help. They freely gave, but this woman was about to learn what God can do with nothing. In fact, it was as if Elisha was saying to her, "You do not yet have enough nothingness, so go borrow all the emptiness you can and see what happens when you really get empty."

Is God interested in cooking oil? Does He care about the basics of life such as cooking supper, making wedding receptions happy, and church picnics that run out of food? He certainly does. Does it matter to Him that I pray for help to pass an examination, find a parking place, or know His will about a small purchase? Indeed it does. He cares about every detail of our life and wants the best for us in each. God meets us at the most common point of our need. Perhaps our problem is that we have too much. In fact, I think it is safe to say that if you are not experiencing God's presence and provision in your life, you may not be empty enough.

I once read the story of a man named Richard who spent fourteen years in Romanian captivity, in solitary confinement because of his faith in Christ. Other Christians were housed in the prison, and in the early years of incarceration they worked out a system of communication by tapping on the sewer pipes. One of the Christian prisoners sent a message to Richard suggesting they celebrate communion. Richard was heartbroken. He would have loved to have communion, but there were no elements to represent the body and blood of Christ. When he tapped out a message explaining the dilemma, he received this reply: "God specializes in taking nothing and making it something; let's have communion." When Richard was released from prison he testified that his most meaningful times were those moments when he pictured the bread in his hands and broke it and tapped to the next cell, "Take and eat in remembrance of me." God always meets us at our most common point of need, and He specializes in our emptiness!

3. The Size of Your Faith Determines the Size of Your Blessing.

The widow's actions showed she believed, but how much did she believe? How many empty pots did she borrow? Thirty? Three hundred? Three thousand? The story doesn't say, but I'm guessing the number was based on the amount of faith she was willing to risk. After all, if the God of Elisha didn't come through, it would simply be more work and more embarrassment to return all those borrowed pots!

We have a faith reservoir inside each of us, and its size determines our capacity for blessing. I once owned a vehicle that had a forty-two gallon gas tank. It took forever to fill up, but the good news was that I could almost travel forever without having to refuel. Wouldn't it be wonderful to develop a faith reservoir that was being continually filled by the presence and provision of God! We can do that when we realize that our Heavenly Father is the giver of all gifts and that He is ready to bless our lives when we reach out to Him in faith. This is the message of Scripture time and time again. Whether it is a little boy's lunch or the water pots at a Galilean wedding reception, God is interested in building our faith. Never forget this: When the widow ran out of pots, the oil stopped flowing. As long as there was something to fill, God kept pouring the oil.

Each believer is a vessel that God can fill to overflowing. The question is simple: Are we empty enough of ourselves to be continually full of Him? Humble yourself each day under the hand of God, rest in His presence, and be in awe of what He does in your life, and through you, in the lives of others.

CHAPTER 19

Gideon

Judges 7:2, 5–7

1. The Tougher the Game, the Greater the Glory.

Gideon found himself living in a very uncomfortable time for both himself and his people. It had not always been that way. He could remember back seven years to a time when Israel was at peace, but now the Midianites oppressed and harassed them every day. Things got so bad the people actually decided to pray! God sent an unknown prophet into the midst of this tough time, but apparently they didn't listen. God didn't give up easily, though; in fact, He never does. Instead He called upon a young farm boy named Gideon and gave him the assignment of taking on the Midianites. To say Gideon was in over his head is an understatement, but with some reluctance Gideon accepted God's call.

Captain Gideon did what anyone in his position would do—he prepared for war. He hoped to recruit enough Israelites to equal the Midianite army, over thirty thousand strong. But God said, "If you win with equal numbers, Israel will take the credit, claiming by her strength she won the victory." God always intends conflict as an opportunity for Him to give the victory. The tougher the game, the greater the glory—to God. God wants glory not to satisfy a thirst for praise and adoration, but to build faith in our lives by lifting our focus beyond ourselves to Him. God demands we give Him glory, not because He needs to receive it, but because we

70

need to give it, and He will purposefully create difficult situations to prove Himself to us.

When Gideon hesitated to accept God's assignment, God asked him a thought-provoking question: "Am I not sending you?" I suggest to you that God walks into our lives every day and asks us the same question. He has some dark places and some tough assignments, and He needs someone like you who understands who is doing the sending. One of the first lessons young police cadets learn in the academy is that the police dispatcher speaks with the authority of the chief of police. Whatever the dispatcher commands, they must immediately obey. Often there is no time to ask why or why not. Someone's life may depend on that officer's immediate response. The key is in understanding who's doing the sending. When God calls, He sends. When God sends us, He provides the opportunity to give Him glory, especially in the most difficult of situations.

2. God Puts First Those Who Put Him First.

Judges 7:5–6 reads, "So Gideon took the men down to the water. There the LORD told him, 'Separate those who lap the water with their tongues like a dog from those who kneel down to drink.' Three hundred men lapped with their hands to their mouths. All the rest got down on their knees to drink."

The faithful three hundred probably did not put their mouth on the surface of the lake to lap up the water. Instead, they filled their hands with water, lifted the water in their hands to their mouth, and lapped it directly from their hands. In that sense they were said to "lap like a dog." This they would have done sitting up. But thousands of others got down on their knees and began to drink. Ten thousand knelt down, thinking about water. Three hundred sat up, thinking about the Lord's battle. Thousands thought about themselves, while only three hundred put the Lord's interest first. They drank with heads held high, looking around for the enemy, watching out for God's interests. Shortly God would perform one of the greatest miracles of all time through just three hundred committed men. What heroes they remain today, thirty-two centuries after the event!

I read recently about a rural church in Kentucky that prided itself in being a training ground for seminary students ministering in their first pastorate. While interviewing a potential pastor, a member of the search committee mentioned the former pastors who had gone on to serve in prominent places—one as pastor of a large metropolitan church, another as a seminary president, a third as a president of two international conventions and an international alliance. "Where in the world did you find this many potentially great men in this little church?" the astonished candidate asked. "Find them!" answered the committee member. "We didn't find them. We made them!" God makes men and women great who put Him first in their lives and seek Him with their whole heart. Perhaps the key comes when we can begin to see ourselves as God sees us. Gideon saw himself as a farmer, but God saw him as a fighter. God called him "Mighty Warrior." Gideon had never heard such words. One of the great tools Satan uses is to convince us we are less than adequate or insignificant. The presumption of inadequacy mocks the wonderful grace of God. It makes a lie out of the Bible. It makes Jesus small in your life. God looked at David and saw not a shepherd, but a king. He looked at Simon Peter and saw not a fisherman, but a preacher.

3. God's Resources Are Always Equal to His Requirements.

The Lord's strategy to win with a mere three hundred men was simple: surround the enemy, swing the lights, blow the horn, break the pitcher, and shout—a simple but effective plan to create confusion. In that atmosphere of distraction and confusion, the Midianites chopped each other to bits. Joshua 7:22 says, "When the three hundred trumpets sounded, the LORD caused the men throughout the camp to turn on each other with their swords."

I believe the Lord will use that same plan at the second coming of Christ. Second Thessalonians 2:8 reminds us that the Lord will destroy the Antichrist and his hosts with "the brightness of His coming." I believe that the dazzling white brilliance of the glory of Jesus Christ will be so blinding, that in the resultant confusion, the armies of Antichrist seeking to annihilate Israel will turn and slay each other. The promise that "God is not the author of confusion" is for the believer. But He often confuses the enemy, and we do well to look for His hand in those times. Even now, when He is "stirring up the nest" He is often very near.

One of the things I love about the story of Gideon is that the angel did not get into a discussion with Gideon about what God had or had not done in the past. He simply promised him that the Lord would provide all he needed. God sent Gideon to do a job, and that's enough. When we are living in the center of God's will, we can depend upon Him to provide every need of our lives. I read these words recently: "The sign of God's presence with you is that your feet are where you did not expect them to be." God may be asking you to do something that makes you uncomfortable even to think about. Perhaps your discomfort is a sign of God's presence and hints at a remarkable mission He has a plan for you, and His resources are always equivalent to the task.

CHAPTER 20

Samson

Judges 16:21–22, 25–30

1. A Moment of Grace Can Erase a Lifetime of Guilt.

The story of Samson's decline is a tragedy of the first order. From beginning to end there is little to applaud. The product of a dysfunctional home, he had nothing but negative earthly relationships. Two times the angel of the Lord came to his parents' home with news and instruction on the impending birth of this very special man. On both occasions the angel bypassed the father and did business with the mother, the obvious head of the home. Little wonder that each of his three female relationships were flawed. Yet in a moment of grace, Samson did more at his death to deliver Israel from her enemies than anything he had accomplished throughout all of his twisted and tortured life. Great and mighty is the grace of our awesome God!

Most of us will never have the opportunity to perform a heroic act at the end of our life, but all of us will leave a legacy. If you came to the end of your earthly journey and had the chance to write words that would be read by your family, friends, and maybe many others, what subject would you choose?

As you consider that question, perhaps it will help to know what three New Testament apostles chose to write about in their final days. Peter, Paul, and John shared a common characteristic; their dependence upon grace. All three chose to write about that grace near the end. Paul wrote in 2 Timothy

4:22, "The Lord be with your spirit. Grace be with you!" Peter wrote in 2 Peter 3:18, "But grow in the grace and knowledge of our Lord and Savior Jesus Christ." And John wrote in Revelation 22:21, "The grace of the Lord Jesus be with all the saints."

Don't you find it incredibly significant that all three of these great Christian leaders close out their lives writing of God's grace? I think the message of Paul's life was simply "grace saves you." And the message of Peter's was "grace keeps you." John's message to us is "grace will take you home." God's grace upon Samson accomplished more at the moment of his death than it had in his entire life.

2. A Man Wrapped Up in Himself Is a Very Small Package Indeed.

Samson was a fierce conqueror who subdued armies using only a donkey's jawbone. He had once taken his wrath out on the Philistines by burning their fields with firebrands made from the tails of foxes. Now the mighty deliverer was confined to a small cell of his own making. Think of the blinded, bound, and shorn Samson, whirling around and around in the same tiny spot, the same tight circle, hooted and ridiculed, smaller and smaller in the eyes of his enemies. His every earthly choice had been made to please himself, and now his life had come to this.

Many persons build prison cells for themselves. No court of law finds them guilty, no judge sentences them to prison, but their dungeon is just as real. In building a lifestyle, they forget to build a life. I saw a sign on a marquee once that said, "The problem with a self-made man is that he worships his creator." In college I remember taking a psychology class in which we learned about the "Johari Window." The Johari Window hypothesis suggests that we all have blind spots we cannot see. Samson had a huge blind spot, and his inability to see his own weakness made him a pawn in the hands of Delilah and turned his blind spot into the real thing.

What of you? Have you any idea of your multiplicity of weaknesses? Have you built into your life an accountability network with trusted friends who will be honest enough to tell you when you are wrong? He who thinks he needs nothing or no one needs more than he can imagine. Remember Samson. Perhaps you have a blind spot too.

3. The Death of Influence Is the Greatest Death of All.

God created and commissioned Samson to make a difference. The Philistines were the most persistent and antagonistic of Israel's enemies and the most consistent imagery of Satan in the Old Testament. When Philistine fathers brought their little children to taunt the once mighty conqueror, he was at the low point of his life, perhaps as low as any hero of the Old Testament; and the loss of his leadership must have seemed worse than death to him.

Several years ago, I saw one of my closest friends in ministry suffer the pain of moral failure. I watched his life slowly tear apart at the seams and eventually crumble. I maintained a relationship with him and always tried to see him each time I traveled to his city. Visiting with him was like watching a man sit among the ruins. Although he found gainful employment, my heart would break every time I walked away from his home. Here was a man who once was a rising star, a charismatic personality with an ever-expanding influence, and it all came crashing down. Yet I am convinced that the greatest tragedy was the death of his influence on others.

In the marvelous prologue to his gospel, the apostle John writes that Jesus, the Word, was the light in a world of darkness, and that the darkness did not comprehend it. Our word *comprehended* is from the Greek word *katalambano*. It means to "down take," and refers to a favorite practice of ancient armies. The strength of Roman cities was their walls. Captured cities were forced to *katalambano*—take down their wall—brick by brick, and walk on pavement made from the rubble, adding insult to the injury of their defeat. Just as a defeated city was a reminder to all that passed by, so is the life of one who has suffered defeat at the hands of our enemy. Satan's enemy is the church and anything he can do to distract, decay, or embarrass her gives him great pleasure. Satan loves to humiliate us and flaunt our failures to the world. The downfalls of the Swaggarts, Bakers, Tiltons, and Jesse Jacksons are an embarrassment to the followers of the Nazarene.

I am told that an important part of training in competitive sports involves studying videotape, looking for the weaknesses of an opponent. Spot the flaw, no matter how small, and the advantage is yours. Need I remind you that our enemy, the Devil, stalks about seeking whom he may devour? He studies our lives, finds where we are vulnerable, and plots to attack at our points of weakness. Take a lesson from the past. The agony of the death of the influence of a Samson or of any Christian leader far exceeds the pain of the physical death itself.

Chapter 21

Ruth

Ruth 1:6–8, 11, 16

1. Divine Relationships Can Greatly Surpass Earthly Kinship.

Though she did nothing heroic or spectacular, Ruth captivates us because her story is one of the great love stories of all time. She was a Moabite who married into a Jewish family. Her in-laws, Eli and Naomi, had two sons who married Moabite women, probably something about which their parents were not too excited. Tragedy struck, and all the men in the family circle died. Naomi decided it was time for her to go home. Widows in her society, especially those with no sons, were in helpless and hopeless straits. Though there was no guarantee things would be better at home in Israel, she decided to return to Bethlehem. Her daughters-in-law decided to go with her, but somewhere along the way Naomi realized these two girls would be outsiders with no friends and no family and told them to go back.

But Ruth would have none of it. Certainly Ruth loved her own birth mother, but she had come to love Naomi, her mother-in-law, with a spiritual and eternal love that binds two persons together in a way beyond human understanding. Only those who share the love of God can forge a bond that is thicker than blood.

I call my two lovely daughters-in-law "daughters-in-love" and love them as I do my own daughter, Ginger. I have come to love hundreds and thousands of wonderful sisters in Christ with a love more real than the love I knew with my own earthly sister. How great is our Lord, to build even greater affections within our relationships as we go through the twists and turns of life! Take inventory of your life and consider the depth of your relationships with Christian brothers or sisters. Maybe this would be a great time to give thanks to God for the beauty of those friendships and then to do something tangible to thank them, too, like sending a note or card expressing the joy that comes from having such a friend.

2. Genuine Commitment to Another Is Commitment to the End of Yourself.

It is not possible in true friendship to tell where one person begins and the other ends. Listen to these words from the lips of Ruth: "Where you go I will go, and where you stay I will stay. Your people will be my people and your God my God." But for Ruth, even that was not enough. Hear the climactic words of affection for her beloved mother-in-law: "Where you die I will die, and there I will be buried." Jesus said in John 15:13, "No one has greater love than this, that someone would lay down his life for his friends." Paul writes in Ephesians 5 that we are to love our wives as Christ loved his bride, the church, even to the point of death.

God intends for human commitments, particularly marriage, to be unending, and there can be no commitment to another without the total giving of oneself. When Ruth promised her mother-in-law she would go where she went, live among her people, and honor her God, she showed herself to be a good woman. When she committed herself to the very end of both their lives, she revealed the *great* woman she truly was.

John D. Rockefeller once wrote, "I believe that every right implies a responsibility, every opportunity an obligation, and every possession a duty." We love to talk about our rights, but we easily overlook our responsibilities. When we stand at the altar of a church to be married or to dedicate our children to God we are assuming rights, but with those rights come tremendous responsibilities. Ruth made a courageous commitment to Naomi, and it was one not easy to make. Naomi was so hurt by how life had turned out, she changed her name to Mara, which means "bitter." She may not have been the easiest person to make a commitment to, but Ruth was willing to give up some of her hopes and dreams because she understood what it meant to make a commitment and live by it.

3. True Love Goes Beyond One's Own Pleasure to Pleasing Another.

Who wouldn't want to marry a beautiful, gracious woman like Ruth? But Boaz, who became God's special man in her life, was not thinking only of himself. What a thoughtful word he spoke when he told his friends he was marrying her, in part that she might raise up children to continue the name of her deceased, beloved first husband. Could it be this awesome act of unselfish love by the man she married was inspired by the selflessness of her own life? I think Ruth's love was contagious; that kind of love almost always is. Spend time with people that love as Ruth loved, and before long you are putting the past behind and celebrating the future. I love the words of Oswald Chambers, "Leave the irreparable past in His hand, and step out into the irresistible future with Him."

If Ruth's story is about anything it is about loyalty: loyalty to a mother-in-law, loyalty to God, loyalty to a new husband. Loyalty is our pledge of allegiance, our promise to stick it out in good times and bad. Loyalty means that if there is war, then we go to war—and if we die, we die. Jesus did not come with a secret society and a hidden agenda. The opportunity is there for all of us to love Him enough to take up our cross daily and follow wherever He chooses to lead. And it means not turning back.

Most everyone has heard of "Ma Bell," the telephone company, but do you know who the real Ma Bell was? The nickname comes from a remarkable story of two women. It seems there was a speech therapist and a schoolteacher who had a deep compassion for deaf children. He drew up plans for an invention that would make sound waves visible, so that deaf people could "see" speech instead of hear it. The invention was a failure, but in the process, he invented the telephone. Alexander Graham Bell was the name of that speech therapist and schoolteacher. There were two Ma Bells in his life. One was also a schoolteacher who encouraged him to pursue his dreams. The other was a young, beautiful, and rich girl named Mabel. Alexander was brilliant but poor, yet he and Mabel overcame all the obstacles and married. These two women in Alexander's life supported, inspired, and encouraged Alexander; yet remarkably, neither could ever really appreciate his invention, for both were deaf. Someone in your life needs to experience unqualified love. Who knows what you might inspire them to do.

CHAPTER 22

Saul

1 Samuel 13:13–14

1. It's What's Inside That Counts.

Saul's picture could have graced the cover of any magazine. Though times were different, some things never change; people have always been attracted to the exterior. The first image of King Saul is of a tall and powerful man, the captain of Israel's army, unsurpassed in his stately regalia. But look on the inside, because that is where God always looks.

Jesse made the same mistake a few years later when Samuel the priest came looking for Saul's replacement. Remember what God told Samuel, "Do not consider his appearance or his height, for I have rejected him. The LORD does not look at the things man looks at. Man looks at the outward appearance, but the LORD looks at the heart" (1 Sam. 16:7). Hundreds of years later we continue to make the same mistake. Television tells us that image is everything, and we buy the message. But God's message to Samuel has not changed. Character still counts.

Twice in my life I made the mistake of inviting powerful looking men to serve on my staff. In each case I knew deep inside that their spiritual qualifications were borderline, but because of their appearance, I reasoned they must have attributes within which were not easily visible. I took a chance, and in both cases was wrong.

Do your remember Monty Hall's television show "Let's Make a Deal"? One of the favorite ploys of the show was to

82

offer a contestant a chance to trade what they had won for the unknown. The key to this ruse was decorating the unknown in a beautifully wrapped package. Occasionally the contestant made a better deal, but most often the trade was a trap. Saul's attractiveness could not conceal his character flaws. Even the external trappings of the office of President of the United States cannot long conceal an absence of true character.

2. No Office Rises Above That Which God Has Ordained.

The office of priest was above every other. For the king to presume to perform the duties of the office of high priest was unacceptable. The role of king was to win the battle, bring back the wealth, and support the vision of the prophet. Trouble lies ahead when we begin to presume. You have heard it said that God loves you and has a wonderful plan for your life. The problem is, so does everyone else. One of the keys to life is distinguishing between other people's plan for your life, your own plan for your life, and God's perfect plan for your life. Scripture suggests that a king was not in God's plan for His children. However, when the Israelites selected a king, God was willing to bless him, but He ordained the office of priest above all others, including the king. Saul's problems came, as ours often do, when he forgot the role and responsibilities uniquely created for him.

It is not the person we honor, but the position in which the Father has placed that person. For King Saul to presume to perform the duties that belonged to the office of the priest was fatal. God places strong importance on His ordained chain of command in government, in the church, and in the home. Romans 13:1–7 reminds us that human leadership is always an extension of God's authority. God established this system, not to punish, but to protect. Work within His plan and watch the promises of His Word become yours!

3. A Passion for God Is the Real Key to Royalty.

Saul was replaced by David, a man "after God's own heart." His passion was serving and pleasing God, whom he loved more than life. What is your passion? That is a question each of us needs to ask and answer. Let me ask another way. What drives you? You can name just about anything and find someone is passionate about it. The sports world is consumed with passion by both player and spectator. As I write these words the Super Bowl has just ended, basketball season is underway, and baseball spring training is just around the corner. Passion about sports extends even to watching them. A well-known recliner manufacturer has begun selling its first reclining chair with a built-in cooler. The "Oasis" only costs $899 and features a thermoelectric cooling unit underneath a flip-up arm pad that can hold up to six twelve-ounce cans. It includes a cup holder, a telephone in the other arm, a ten-speed massager, and heating system.

Your passion may not be sports. It may be a job, a relationship, or a hobby. Oprah Winfrey did an entire show recently entitled "Turning Your Passion Into Profit." She interviewed people who were passionate about gardening, cake decorating, shoes, and linens, as well as a man who gave up his law practice to go into the mustard business. One of her guests was an expert on passion. She said, "Expressing your passion is your best chance at happiness!" So do a little self-inventory: What is your passion? What drives you?

Ask yourself the question: Am I willing to die for my passion? Jesus was. Jesus knew that everyone has one controlling passion that ultimately shapes everything else in their life. He said: "For where your treasure is, there your heart will be also" (Matt. 6:21). He knew that our passion controls our perspective and orients our priorities. God created us to have one controlling passion. That passion influences our perspective and our priorities—how we spend our time, talents, and treasures.

Saul didn't have a passion for God, so his perspective was distorted and his priorities were out of place. Being born a king does not make one kingly. God did not tear the kingdom from the hand of Saul and give it to another because He wanted a better warrior or even a better king, but because He wanted a better man. Saul's successor may not have looked like a king, but the Bible says "He was a man after God's own heart." What a great epitaph for a life! Begin cultivating a real passion for God today and enjoy the royal privilege of living as a child of the king should live!

CHAPTER 23

David

1 Samuel 17:32-40

1. Problem Solving Requires the Proper Perspective.

Charlie Brown says, "No problem facing our nation is so awesome, so complicated, or so fraught with danger that the average citizen can't run away from it." The story of David and Goliath is a story about a nation of average citizens who were running away. Those who grew up in church have sung songs about the story, seen flannelgraph presentations, and listened to it taught scores of times. It is a story with great appeal because it has an underdog. In fact, if there was ever an underdog, it was the shepherd boy David going up against the giant Goliath. Can you imagine the odds the David-Goliath fight would have gotten in Las Vegas? The question wasn't when David was going to be knocked out, but where to hold the funeral. But David had a unique perspective—God's!

His brothers saw only the sword that was in Goliath's hand. David saw the sling that was in *his* hand. His brothers felt intimidated because no one had ever fought a giant like this before. The boy David felt confident because he had already fought and vanquished both bear and lion. God had protected him against an enemy much larger than Goliath. He would give him strength once again.

When you face a problem, back off and look at it, size it up, and ask some questions. Have not such problems been solved before? What greater problem has God already solved for you? Is it as big as God? Look at the greatness of your God. To a boy, a bear was a bigger obstacle than a giant was to an army. What David's God had done before, he knew He could do again.

All of us come across giants in our life. Our Goliath may be physical, emotional, financial, or spiritual. The giant may come in the form of a person, a situation, or even a memory. Facing giants is always an intimidating experience, but it all changes when we gain God's perspective. Saul and his troops looked at Goliath through human eyes—they saw the giant as too big to hit. David, through God's eyes, saw Him as *too big to miss.* Got any giants in your life? Stop looking at the giants and start looking at God.

2. Great Opportunity Lies in the Ordinary.

David didn't set out to be a hero or to pick a fight, let alone one with a giant like Goliath, a fight that would enshrine him in the hearts of God's people forever. He merely went to the battleground to take food to his brothers. Life's great victories exist in one's everyday opportunities. Those who recite the verse, "Thou hast been faithful over a little, I will make you ruler over much" need to give more attention to the *faithfulness* of the little than the potential of the much.

Consider the contrasts in the story. On one side we have Goliath, a champion, nine feet tall with a bronze helmet, one hundred and twenty-five pounds of armor, fifteen-pound spear point, bronze javelin, bronze leggings, and a shield bearer in front. On the other hand we have David, a shepherd boy carrying a staff, a pouch, a sling, and five smooth stones. David lived an ordinary life and armed himself with ordinary things.

It's easy to get caught up in the ordinary and in the process miss the extraordinary. God sightings are all around us, we just need the right perspective. Take some time to examine an ordinary day. Make a list of the places where you have been and the people you have seen. Was God at work? Did you miss Him because you weren't looking? Can you see some places where He might be at work? Even more importantly, is there somewhere in your ordinary day in which He might use you to do His work?

3. Fight in Your Own Armor and Let Others Do So as Well.

King Saul was not willing to fight Goliath, but he was willing to lend David his armor. David refused the invitation. Not only did it fit poorly, he didn't need it. God would protect him. What Saul did comes quite naturally to many of us. Our temptation is to put our armor on someone else. We expect one child to act like the other. We want our new boss to be just like the old one we loved so much. Unfortunately, these expectations are a prescription for disappointment and maybe even disaster. The reverse is true, as well. We see someone we admire or we follow in someone's footsteps, and the temptation to put on their armor is just too great. We need to walk in our own armor and let others do so as well.

David was faithful to hone those skills that came naturally to him. Our Lord only expects the employment of the natural gifts He has placed within our hands. God's question is always, "What are you going to do with what you've got?" Whether it is a staff, a lunch, an empty net or a sling, God doesn't ask for very much at all. He just asks for all of you. Five smooth stones will do just fine.

God has gifted each of us and placed in our hands the gifts we may most naturally and successfully employ. How do you know your spiritual gift? By looking at two areas of your life: What comes naturally to you, and what you do that God blesses. How would our Lord have you approach your ministry? The answer lies within God's gift of that slingshot you hold in your hand.

CHAPTER 24

Jonathan

1 Samuel 8:1; 20:1–2, 17

1. God Raises Up Deliverance from Unlikely Sources.

What is the most extravagant expression of love you have ever received? Was there ever a time someone did something for you that you will never forget? Just a few years ago the newspapers were abuzz with a remarkable story. Carlos Rogers of the Toronto Raptors, now a Houston Rocket, was doing an incredible thing. He had worked long and hard to make it to the NBA. His future, all the benefits he had worked for, were right before him. Now he was possibly throwing it all away. Why? Carlos's sister was sick, very sick. She could not survive without a new kidney. Carlos Rogers left his position in the NBA to go home and donate one of his kidneys to his sister. He knew it would end his career, but compared to his love for his sister, he didn't care. *USA Today* called Carlos Rogers "the most unselfish man in the NBA."

Receiving help from a brother or sister might not be unexpected, but when King Saul attempted yet another time to slay David, it was Saul's own son who saved David. Jonathan risked his own life and future by reaching out to save the life of his friend. Can you see the picture? It looks forward to generations later, when from the house of David came the Messiah. What powerful symbolism of the guilty sinner running from the anger of God while salvation exists in the Son of that very one from whom we flee!

For many years we lived next door to a family who desperately despised us because of the Gospel. In spite of our efforts and prayers, they remained hostile to anything related to the Savior. In my heart I am confident one day they will turn to the one from whom they flee, and as the spies found help from Rahab, they will ask us to help them find the Lord. May we look again at the gloved hand of the God we so much fear? For inside it is a gentle touch of love to lead us to the Father. Like the prodigal, when we come to our senses and take the first step toward home, we find a God that runs to receive us as His beloved.

2. True Friends Place Friendship Above All Else.

Count it a real blessing if you are fortunate to have one or two intimate friendships in this life. Friends like these can be counted on and called on. They help you celebrate the victories of your life and stand by your side in your darkest defeats. Find a friend like this, then give thanks to God for the special gift He has provided.

The story of David and Jonathan is a story of the gift of friendship. No family ties, loyalties, or blood kinship could surpass the loyalty of these true friends. The souls of Jonathan and David were knit to the death. And no ugliness, sin, failure, or flaw of David could shake Jonathan's loyalty to him or make him love him less. If a friend is anything, it is someone who knows everything about you and loves you nonetheless. The hymn writer said it well, "Jesus! What a Friend to Sinners." When others forsake you and your own family deserts you, Jesus will be a friend that sticks closer than a brother.

Jesus had a friend who poured out expensive perfume and never seemed to give a second thought to the extravagance of the gift. Friends do extravagant things for their friends. Can you think of a time when a friend did something special that he or she didn't have to do and wasn't expected to do? If you've had that wonderful experience you won't soon forget it.

Maybe you have received a special blessing because your friend did one of these:

- She traveled out of her way because she cared.
- He stayed the night with you in a quiet hospital room.
- She gave you a gift that touched you to the core of your being.
- He met a need that seemed impossible.

Frequent expressions of love are like oxygen to us—we need them to survive. But those extraordinary acts of love come into our memories again and again, and we enjoy their sweet aroma over and over.

3. True Friendship Knows No Earthly Limitation or Eternal Boundaries.

Well beyond the end of Jonathan's life, David was looking for ways to express his love to his long departed friend. One day he dispatched his servants with the charge to find any living relative of Jonathan in all the kingdom. They returned to say that a small, crippled boy, a distant nephew of Jonathan, was the only one to be found. In an act of great love, David sent for the boy, Mephibosheth, and adopted him into his family in honor of his long deceased friend, Jonathan. No proclamations were read, no headlines filled the front pages of the Jerusalem newspapers. It was just a simple act, born quite naturally out of the heart of love of a man whose love for his friend knew no limitations, even the grave. Real friendship is like that, and blessed is the person who has such a friend. One such friend wants to know you and adopt you into His family this very day.

A few years ago a young doctoral student moved in with a Navajo family as a part of the research for his dissertation. For a year he lived with the family on a reservation in the Southwest, sleeping in their hogan, eating their food, and working with them to document life for the twentieth-century Native American. The grandmother in the family spoke no English, but during the course of the year she forged a special friendship with the young student. Their shared language of love made up for the spoken language differences they faced. As the year passed he learned a few Navajo words and she picked up some words in English. When his research was complete and the time came for him to return to school, the village held a going-away party, for he had become a wonderful friend. On the day of departure the grandmother stood by his pickup truck and with broken English said, "I like me best when I am with you." What a powerful description of what a friend brings to our life!

One of the great questions of life is this: Whom do you love? If you have any questions at all about who or what you love, ask a friend. The friend can tell you. You cannot hide love. It shows up in all kinds of places—obvious places like your face, the tone of your voice, your calendar, and your checkbook. Who or what you love is not hard to figure out. Your family knows, your friends know, your neighbors and coworkers might even know. We have a hard time hiding what we love. David could not hide his love for Jonathan, and God cannot hide His love for you. He loved you so much that He sent His only Son to die on a cross, that He might spend eternity with you.

CHAPTER 25

Bathsheba

2 Samuel 11:2–5

1. Seldom Is Only One Responsible for the Sins of Two.

Sin never occurs in a vacuum. Despite the old argument that no one will get hurt, people always do; and more often than not, the consequences of sin are widespread, hurting the guilty and innocent alike. The story of David and Bathsheba's affair sounds more like an episode from a soap opera than something out of the Bible, but God is faithful to give us the whole picture, even when it is not very pretty. Evidently, Bathsheba was not the aggressor, but while we hold leaders accountable for their sin and often discount the other party, it still takes two to tango. In no way can Bathsheba be pronounced fully innocent in her affair with David.

Uriah, Bathsheba's husband, was an officer in Israel's army. Bathsheba lived on the post. She had friends among the enlisted men and their wives. She knew where the quarters were, the mess hall, and certainly the residence of the commander-in-chief. Could she possibly have not known where the king's palace was, where the balcony was located and where the king took his daily walk? I ask three questions:

1. Do people normally take showers in the evening rather than in the morning?
2. Who bathes in public view and not in private?
3. If he could see her, could she not see him?

93

With hundreds of square miles in Israel, how did she happen to choose those four square feet? I really don't like the sound of the statement, "And David sent messengers and took her." What does that mean? Was there a command? Was she constrained or even forced? And yet while David was clearly in the wrong, was the entire situation exacerbated by a temptress who knew precisely what she was doing? We hear much about the innocent party. It is highly likely, however, that few, in fact, exist.

We are confronted every day with the opportunity to choose between good and evil. Quite often the evil doesn't seem as bad if everyone is doing it, especially someone in a position of authority and leadership. Their example is an influence, albeit a negative one, and their poor choices may seriously impact the decisions of us all. But never forget that each of us will answer for our own sin. Someone has defined integrity as "what you are when no one is looking." David was looking, but so perhaps was Bathsheba—and their sin led to heartache and death.

2. Sin's Consequences Are Most Often Shared.

Before-and-after pictures are one of the most effective forms of advertising. I've often wondered how much pain would be avoided if people could see a picture or watch a video depicting the aftermath of their sin. It would not be a very appealing picture because no one wants to look ahead. The pleasure of the moment consumes the voice of the conscience, and potential pain is stuffed away with the delusion that it will never come. But it always does.

David should have been at war. It was that time of year, but instead he was home, and probably bored. Bathsheba should have been more modest, but her husband was off at war, and perhaps found herself in need of a new adventure. Did either of them want to deal with a funeral? No, they simply wanted to have fun, but their moments of pleasure led to years of pain.

Much has been said of David's heartbreak over the death of his child, but what about a mother's grief, as well? That precious little boy was Bathsheba's baby too. The residue of sin ripples through the life of everyone it touches and beyond. Through the years I have watched both women and men make decisions that would later cause tremendous regret. And not just decisions made in the passion of a moment, but choices considered for weeks and sometimes even months. Unfortunately, God was nowhere in the picture. No prayers were prayed, no counsel apparently sought. Ultimately, they did what they wanted to do. That's what happened with Bathsheba. That's what happened with David. Neither would tell you the price that they paid was worth it.

3. God's Mighty Grace Allows for Second Chances.

David's confession consists of only six short words: "I have sinned against the Lord." God, the God of grace, accepted David's confession. While David had committed adultery and murder, and had been involved in a cover-up that made Watergate look like a grade school play, he repented and made a decision to serve the Lord. We are left to ponder whether Bathsheba repented, as well. David comforted his wife Bathsheba, and God gave them another son, this time of a legitimate union—an honored birth of a boy named Solomon, who would become the wisest man who ever lived. The narrative tells us that as they embraced each other through the night, weeping over the loss of their son, David and Bathsheba conceived Solomon. Had that long night of weeping, comforting, and sharing not occurred because of the death of the baby, would we have the books of Proverbs, Song of Solomon, and Ecclesiastes? Truly the lengthening shadow of God's grace far exceeds His judgment.

Do you need a second chance? None of us outgrow the need for God's saving, sanctifying, and sustaining grace in our lives. Over the years I have met both men and women who were absolutely convinced they could not be forgiven, usually because they could not forgive themselves. What a comfort to take them to Scripture and show them the story of people like Rahab, the prostitute, and Bathsheba, the adulteress, and many others who found forgiveness from our loving God of the second chance.

CHAPTER 26

Esther

Esther 4:12–14

1. When God Does Something It Is as Important as What He Does.

Most people journey through life talking about fate, chance, or luck that puts them in the right place at the right time. God's children take a different journey, for we know He ordains the days of our lives before we are born. While Esther is the only book in the Bible that does not mention God's name, His presence is clearly there, and this classic story is a message of His great providence. Providence comes from two Latin words: *pro,* which means "before," and *video,* which means "to see." The meaning is powerful; God sees events before they happen.

Esther is an amazing book, and Queen Esther was a remarkable woman. Prior to this point in Jewish history, we have seen a God that has done the bold and the big, parting large bodies of water, sending multiple plagues, burning bushes, and causing great storms. But the book of Esther portrays a God who chooses to work through a few gentle and obedient hearts to save His chosen people. Esther was not the first, nor would she be the last to be in a critical place at a critical time. And what of you? Have you given serious thought to the time in which God has called you to live? Have you considered that there are people's lives that may not be saved if you fail God's purpose for your life?

If I have found anything to be important in nearly fifty years of Christian ministry it is this: Timing is everything with God. Who can forget those incredible words of Mordecai to Esther, encouraging her to speak a word of truth that could save thousands of lives from death—"And who knows but that you have come to royal position for such a time as this?" What were the chances that a beautiful queen, quiet and unassuming, would be God's instrument to save the Jews, as did Joseph down in Egypt? But she happens to find herself, as did he, to be the right person in the right place at the right time to save the entire Jewish nation, through whom the Savior of the world was to come. If she had failed, much more would have been lost than ever the human mind could fathom.

When you miss a plane, find a meeting postponed, or come across circumstances rearranged beyond your control, relax and praise the Lord! God is getting ready to do something in your life that must be hurried or delayed in connection with the rest of His entire schedule. He is only slowing down or speeding up to bring you to a divine appointment. Relax in His timetable. It's a terrific way to live.

2. Miss God's Timing and You Miss God's Best.

"Esther," said Mordecai, "This is your time, your destiny, for which you were born. For this divine moment in history, you stand in this royal position in this palace. Right here— right now! Miss God's purpose and miss the golden moment in time for which you were born. If you do nothing, remember that help will come from another source." The great honor and esteem in which history holds Esther would have gone to another. Esther had a choice. We always do. That is the great gift humans received from God at creation. How many times have you known God's will and chosen to go another way? While Esther's choice appeared to put her life in great danger, God's plan meant that her life and the lives of her people would be saved.

One person can make a difference, but the old song is right, "One is the Loneliest Number." Esther, with the counsel of Mordecai, came to understand the importance of her role in the salvation of the Jews. Edward Everett Hale once wrote, "I am only one. But still I am one. I cannot do everything. But still I can do something. And because I cannot do everything I will not refuse to do the something I can do." What is the one thing you can do? Maybe it is to pray or give resources to God's work. Perhaps it is volunteering in a hospital or visiting a nursing home. Never let what you cannot do keep you from doing what you can do.

Here's a friendly reminder: God's master plan will be accomplished with or without you. Miss His purpose and you will miss His blessing. That privilege in God's eternal plan, that moment in time, that place in Christian history, will go to another. How sad! Much is lost when we run ahead of God, or lag behind. His perfect timing is everything. There are no sadder words than these: "It might have been."

3. God's Best for You Exceeds Your Wildest Imagination.

Have you discovered that God's plan is both calculated and creative? He does not wake up in a new world every morning wringing His hands and wondering what's next! When Captain Scott O'Grady's F–16 plane was shot down over Serbia, America waited and wondered if our pilot had been killed or captured. On the sixth day, another pilot detected a faint radio message with the downed pilot's position. Immediately the Marines launched a daring rescue operation and snatched Captain O'Grady to safety by helicopter. *Newsweek* reported a startling statistic: the value of all the weapons and machinery risked to save our soldier's life was estimated at six billion dollars! Need I remind you that this figure pales in comparison to what God spent to save yours?

Esther's story is just one in a long line of God sightings, stepping in at the right time and with the right person to see His people protected. If this timid Jewish girl had been afraid to speak, or too shy to say anything to the king, the results would have been inconceivable and devastating. What was at stake? Not only the survival of the Jewish people, but the birth of the Savior, the church, the apostles, and the kingdom of God on earth. Jesus would be born more than five hundred years after her decision but without her willingness to act, there may have been no birth at all. We can never imagine the far-reaching ramifications of simple obedience. Never, never resist the gentle nudge of the Holy Spirit to trust and to act.

Tennyson once wrote, "More things are wrought by prayer than this world dreams of." Have you ever thought about how the Berlin Wall fell? A *Christianity Today* article, "Revolution by Candlelight," states that many people believe the fall of the Berlin Wall came about by prayer. For ten years Christians in Leipzig, East Germany, gathered at a church to pray for the fall of the Wall. In the final months before the breakdown of communism and the collapse of the Wall, thousands of Christians gathered to pray daily, some of the meetings spilling over into gigantic demonstrations. God always has a plan, and that plan always includes faithful, obedient people.

CHAPTER 27

Daniel

Daniel 5:11, 13, 16–17, 28

1. Even the Wicked Recognize and Respect the Godly.

Every single one of us has influence, and we should ask three questions on a regular basis: Who am I influencing? What kind of influence am I? Where will my influence lead? Former professional football player Bubba Smith was making big dollars appearing in commercials for a major beer company. He had no idea what kind of influence he was having until he returned to his alma mater, Michigan State University, and heard the college students hollering out lines from his commercial. Though he personally did not drink the beer, he was shocked by the reception he received during his weekend at Michigan State. When the weekend was over, he called his agent to tell him he would no longer be a spokesperson for the beer company. His reason was simple: "I did not know what it was doing to the kids." By definition, influence is the "act or power of producing an effect without apparent force or direct authority."

Daniel qualifies as one of the world's all-time great influencers. Living in captivity, he had no apparent direct influence, but light always shines in darkness. The fifth chapter of Daniel may well be entitled, "When God Broke Up the Party." When the fingers of a human hand wrote some strange words on the wall as the great King Belshazzar gave a drunken party for a thousand of his lords and ladies, the king was frightened. No one could interpret the prophecy—

not the Chaldeans, soothsayers, astrologers, magicians, or Babylonian wise men—not one person he summoned. Then the queen said, "There is a man in the kingdom who has the spirit of the holy gods in him." What an awesome testimony—and from a pagan queen! How did she know that? Had she ever heard him preach? Listen to him on the radio? Been to his church? No. She had seen his life and stood in awe. He had been an influence.

If there were a horrible tragedy in your school and numbers of young people lay dying as at Columbine, would the teacher say, "Quick, run and get John," or "Go find Mary. There is at least one Christian in this school." When someone in your office experiences a crisis, do they come to you for counsel or to bring a prayer request? The Bible does not say "they will know we are Christians by our loudness," but by our fruit. When you are a Christian, a real Christian, you don't have to flaunt it or advertise it. People will know, and they will respect you and the Christ who lives within you.

Note that Daniel was not *at* the party. He had to be summoned *to* the party. There is a fine line between our separation from the sinner and our love for him, which makes palatable God's love within us. It is a line Daniel walked masterfully. In the world, but not of the world, and certainly not condemning the world, is the attitude that wins for those who would have influence with sinners.

2. Without God, He Who Thinks He Has Everything Has Nothing.

In verse 28 Daniel interprets the prophecy written by the hand on the wall: "Your kingdom is divided and given to the Medes and Persians." In spite of having just heard the prophecy that he would soon have no kingdom left to give, Belshazzar pronounces Daniel third ruler in the kingdom. History records that the Medes and Persians were, that very night, finishing the job of building the tunnel beneath the moat that secured the palace of Belshazzar. Before the party was over, the enemy emerged from the floor beneath and slaughtered King Belshazzar, his lords, generals, captains, and court in less than an hour. How sad. Remember those words, "Without the Lord, he who thinks he has everything in fact has nothing."

Do you know the story of Millard and Linda Fuller? Millard was an attorney and businessman who had it all—multiple houses, matching Lincoln Continentals, designer clothes, and beautiful jewelry. Millard Fuller was the world's example of a self-made man. Despite all his success, however, he found his life empty and his marriage on the brink of collapse. As he and his wife began to discuss divorce, God dealt with him one night in a dream.

In the dream, he gave away all his wealth and began to invest in the lives of other people. When he shared his dream with his wife, she told him she had the same dream. They knew something was happening in their lives. Instead of divorcing, they made a new commitment to each other and began to divest themselves of their fortune. The year was 1968. In 1976, Millard and Linda Fuller settled in Americus, Georgia, and founded Habitat for Humanity. This organization is an ecumenical Christian housing ministry that seeks to eliminate poverty housing by building affordable homes with the help of individuals, churches, businesses, and the homeowners themselves. Today Habitat has 1,150 affiliates across the United States and operates in forty-five countries of the world. The organization has built more than eleven thousand homes in the United States and over thirty thousand worldwide. At one time Millard Fuller had millions of dollars but was miserable. Today he oversees an organization that handles ten times as much money and gives it away. And he's happy!

Do you manage your possessions, or do they manage you? Belshazzar failed to understand what Daniel knew: God owns it all, and we are on earth to be his managers. God wants us to partner with Him. Without Him we merely struggle through life, amusing ourselves with accomplishments that neither last nor satisfy. Millard Fuller will tell you that all the possessions in the world will never make you happy, but discover a relationship and partnership with God and watch what happens.

3. He Who Is Truly a Man of God Cannot Be Bought and Sold.

Commitment makes all the difference in life. I read this powerful statement about commitment a few years ago. "Until I am committed there is a hesitancy, a chance to draw back. But the moment I definitely commit myself, God moves, and a whole stream of events erupt. All manner of unforeseen incidents, meetings, persons, and material possessions which I could never have dreamed possible, begin to flow toward me." God commits Himself to committed people. When we come to crossroads in life, we either confirm or compromise our commitment to God. Every time Daniel reached one of those moments, God honored the confirmation of his commitment. Daniel could not be bought or sold, and everyone knew it.

In verse 17 Daniel refuses the awards and gifts of Belshazzar, saying politely but firmly, "Keep your presents for yourself and give your rewards to another." He knew the possessions of the king were not his to give, and he had no interest in a paper kingdom. Belshazzar's days were over, his kingdom finished; and regardless of the rewards, real or imagined, the man of God was not interested. Proverbs speaks eloquently of the virtuous woman whose value and worth are above price. How refreshing to know there are such men, as well.

Daniel's firm conviction and commitment to God was a testimony to four different Babylonian kings. It was just such a commitment that led King Darius to say in the sixth chapter, "For he is the living God and he endures forever; his kingdom will not be destroyed, his dominion will never end. He rescues and he saves." Quite a speech from a pagan king.

In June 1985, Captain John Testrake endured a seventeen-day ordeal as the pilot of hijacked TWA flight 847. During

the drama, the media reported the words he spoke as he
leaned out the cockpit window with an Uzi machine gun bar-
rel at his head: "The Lord has taken very good care of us so
far, and He's seen us through some trying times and He'll see
us through to the end." Years before, John Testrake had put
his faith in God, and over the years had endured a number of
tragedies, including the death of two of his children and his
wife. In an hour of great need, he found the grace of God sufficient and could not be bought, sold, or threatened. No
price, no compromise, no shame.

CHAPTER 28

Jonah

Jonah 1:1–4, 15

1. Your Arms Are Too Short to Box with God.

Anger creates all kinds of problems, and can even cost you your life. Every year hundreds of people across the United States die as the result of road rage. One person cuts off another in traffic, and before you know it someone decides to settle it with a pistol. Most people would not consider Jonah an angry man, but that's only because they haven't read the whole book. God called Jonah to preach repentance to the wicked city of Nineveh, and he headed straight for Joppa to catch a boat for Tarshish. Why Tarshish? Because Tarshish, or Tinland, known today as Great Britain, was the farthest place in the known world from where he was. Did he really think he could run from God? Did he really believe that God's arm was too short to reach him there? Did the prodigal really believe God would never find him hidden away among the prostitutes and the bars? And what of us? Do we really think we can outsmart Him, force Him out of our lives, and forever do as we please? The Psalmist said it well when he wrote, "If I make my bed in hell, behold thou art there" (Ps. 139:8 KJV).

What are you hiding from today? Where are you running? This morning our little grandson, River John, was playfully hiding behind a large vase in the dining room, arms and legs sticking out on both sides. He was squealing with delight because he really thought since he couldn't see us, we couldn't see him. Adam and Eve tried to hide in the garden and while they were the first, they would not be the last. Down through the ages men and women have attempted to hide from God, but it doesn't matter whether it's the back side of a desert or the darkness of a cave. God always knows where we are, and He always wins. You cannot win the war, you cannot be victorious in the game, and you will lose. Why would we not surrender to the one who loves us so! There is great danger in ignoring what we know to be true.

Jonah knew God was gracious, compassionate, slow to anger, and abounding in love. He knew it in his head but wasn't experiencing it in his heart. Isn't that what anger does to us? We know what is right, but we ignore it. We rationalize, we justify, and we do whatever it takes, because we simply want our way. Put a *d* in front of anger and you have "danger," which is exactly what we get when we live contrary to God's great will.

2. Your Footprints Are Much Deeper Than You Think.

According to the oldest charts of the ancient mariners, the deepest spot in the ocean on the voyage Jonah would have taken to Tarshish is today still called "Running Man." It is more than nine thousand feet deep and is a compelling argument for the veracity of one of the most disbelieved stories in the Bible. Surely ancient tradition marked it as the place of Jonah's battle with the seaweed at the bottom of the ocean. Three thousand years from today will some map mark the site of a spiritual catastrophe in your life because you, too, ran from the will of God? Perhaps not. But in your children and grandchildren, and for generations after them, you will find the imprint of your life to be far deeper than ever you can imagine!

Jonah made the mistake of thinking his disobedience was a private matter. How many times have I talked to people who thought no one else would get hurt by the poor choices they were making! There is a biblical principle from Genesis to Revelation that when you don't allow God to be in control of your life, it will affect those around you, especially those closest to you, for decades. Someone once said the only difference between Christ *running* my life and me *ruining* my life is the letter *I*. God calls us to let Him have complete control of our lives and to live in the world, but not be of the world. And He has given us the Holy Spirit to renew our minds. Norman Vincent Peale tells the story of visiting with the shopkeeper of a tattoo parlor in Hong Kong. Dr. Peale learned the most popular tattoo was one that said "born to lose." In broken English, the shopkeeper told him his customers had the tattoo on their mind before they ever had it on their body. Generation after generation can be tattooed with a negative spirit because of the influences of persons who mistakenly thought they were not hurting anyone but themselves.

Conversely, the same is true with the good we do. On a warm Sunday afternoon in 1856, a shoe cobbler named Edward Kimble led D. L. Moody to Christ. Moody's preaching touched the heart of F. B. Meyers, who led J. W. Chapman to the Lord. Mr. Chapman would open the Chicago Rescue Mission where Billy Sunday would be saved, and ultimately lead Mordecai Hamm to faith in Christ. Under the preaching of Mordecai Hamm, a North Carolina mountain boy named Billy Graham found the Lord. Jonah was the Billy Graham of his day. He had a powerful voice with lots of influence—until God asked him to do something contrary to what he wanted.

None of us have a hard time doing what God wants us to do when it coincides with what we want to do. But what happens when God calls us to use our influence for Him in some places or with some people whom we are not excited about ministering to? What would you do if God called you as a missionary to Iraq or Libya? In essence, that is exactly what God was calling Jonah to do. We act in strange ways when God gives us an assignment we do not like. What might God be calling you to do today? Will you say yes to Him, and will you leave a mark on the map of your tomorrow that eternally imprints the life of another?

3. All of Creation Is against the Man Who Is against God.

The storm blows, the seas rage, and even the pagan sailors realize a rebel is aboard their ship. Cast over the side, he plummets to the bottom of the ocean, tangled in seaweed at what he calls "the roots of the mountains." There, at last, the reluctant prophet prays. Strange that we humans often choose to pray as a last resort instead of a first option! How different things might have been for Jonah if he had simply chosen to talk to God instead of running from Him! Swallowed by a great fish that eventually becomes nauseated by the presence of the backslidden preacher in his stomach, Jonah is vomited out on the shore.

Body, mind, heart, and soul—everything is out of sync when you are out of tune with God. To be against Him is to be against the forces of the universe. On the road to Damascus, Christ said to Saul of Tarsus, "How long will you kick against the goads?" A goad is a pointed rod used to urge on an animal, and it probably worked like the electrical shock sticks used today to herd cattle. When you are against God your soul is in agony, your mind in distress, your home unstable, your finances in disarray, and your judgment clouded. But let God's power flow through you, and everything changes. The safest place in the world is wherever God wants you, and the most dangerous place is out of His will.

Go to the shore of a mighty ocean and place an everyday soda fountain straw horizontally against the tide. It will instantly be crushed and ruined. But place the straw in harmony with the incoming waves and experience the power of the ocean in your hand as it rushes through the straw. God will never let you disobey Him without letting you know, and remember that if you are in the wrong place, then the right place is empty.

A ship was once sold at auction in San Diego because there were no heirs to lay claim to it. Named the *Invader*, this beautiful custom-made boat was built in Quincy, Massachusetts in 1905 for a man named William Borden. Borden had one son who received every advantage throughout his youth. Young Borden was frequently reminded he was going to inherit and run the family business, and his father wanted him to begin preparing himself. Soon after he arrived at college, some friends introduced him to Jesus Christ. His dreams changed, and he announced to his parents he was going to the Orient to be a missionary. They could not believe he was giving up the status, power, and wealth of the family, especially the beautiful family yacht. Mr. Borden tried everything to dissuade his son, but to no avail.

Finally, in desperation William Borden tried to scare his son about the plague that was spreading across the Orient. But nothing worked. His mind was made up, and young Borden would follow God's plan for his life and go to China. Within a few months his parents received a notice from the Mission Board of his death. He had, indeed, died of the plague. Several weeks later, a small package arrived with his personal effects. Included in the package was his Bible. One week prior to his death, he had written on the back leaf of the Bible these words: "No Reserve . . . No Retreat . . . No Regret." Can you say that today? Walking with God is the most exciting, most challenging, and most rewarding experience an individual can ever embrace, and the trip is always first class. Don't miss it! Go against God and die. Go with Him—and live!

Part 3
Principles from
New TestamentCharacters

CHAPTER 29

Mary

Luke 1:26–27, 30–31, 34–35, 37

1. Don't Be Surprised When God Surprises You.

Imagine Mary's surprise when the angel gave to her the assignment as Jesus' earthly mother. Two thousand years later, we still marvel at God's choice of a young teenager to be the mother of our Savior. Wouldn't it have made more sense to have selected an older woman? Surely many other women could have fulfilled the Old Testament prophecy. But God is a God of surprises, and He loves to take ordinary people and ordinary things and make them extraordinary.

Think about it. Our creative God seldom does the same thing, the same way, twice in a row. The Savior of the world was born of a quiet Palestinian girl who was also a virgin. Wow! The announcement to the shepherds, not to the kings, the birth in a manger, not in a palace, the ride on a donkey, not on a white horse pale by comparison to the virgin birth of our Savior. What chance is there that mere mortals could ever have imagined such a setting for the birth of God's son? There is no chance at all. So you feel shock or even unbelief when hearing the Bible account? You don't if you understand that our exciting and creative God loves to act in fresh new ways in the lives of His children. He who designs every snowflake differently, who makes every fingerprint unique, can hardly be expected to do less.

All this means that we should keep our eyes open for a fresh new surprise from our awesome God. He loves to thrill

His children. When He leads you to the unlikely and you find yourself in the midst of the unexpected, look up. Something big may be just around the corner. God chose Mary not because of her education, for she apparently had little; He chose her not for her wealth, because she was likely poor. And He certainly did not choose her for her maturity, because she was very young. God chose Mary because she trusted Him enough to let Him use her. How about you? Do you trust God enough to let Him surprise you? You'll be glad you did. His ways and His surprises are always filled with blessing.

2. Absolutely Nothing Is Too Hard for God.

One day Linus and Charlie Brown were talking about their problems. Linus said, "I don't like to face problems head on. I think the best way to solve problems is to avoid them. In fact, it is a distinct philosophy of mine. No problem is so big or so complicated that it can't be run away from!" Lots of us would embrace Linus' solution to the problems of life. But running away from problems is never the solution. Mary could have seen her situation as a problem, but she chose to see it as a promise filled with all sorts of wonderful possibilities. The angel had assured her that nothing was too hard for God.

What seems hard for us, even impossible, is nothing for Him. People often ask about life on other planets. When I respond that I don't believe there is life there, they ask, "Then why did God go to all that trouble?" My response is simply, "What trouble?" There are no degrees of difficulty with God. No big thing is harder for Him than a small thing. In spite of a problem seeming difficult from our perspective, there are no degrees of difficulty from God's. Nothing is hard, harder, or hardest with Him. The psalmist said, "It is nothing with Him wither with the small or great." Whatever the size of the problem, whatever difficulty you face, remember that it is just as easy for the God who makes babies with men and women a million times a day to create babies from women without men. Our problems, whether minute or monumental, are not problems at all to God.

When we face particularly difficult problems, we start to worry about what we can do, how much it will cost, or how long it will take to get it all worked out. We need to be reminded on a regular basis that God never frets and God never worries. There is no panic switch in heaven. Consider how big a problem the sin of the world was, and then think about the amazing plan God created to solve our plight. The same God arranged the stars provided the Savior. The next time you are tempted to be discouraged by the anxieties of life, remember you have a Heavenly Father who says, "Nothing is impossible for me." Be encouraged.

3. God Will Stop at Nothing to Accomplish His Will in Us.

Mary discovered that God had a plan, custom-made just for her. His plan for our lives is not automatic, but when we cooperate with His purpose He can use us beyond our greatest imagination. Did Gideon expect to go from a farmer to a fighter, David from a shepherd to a king, Paul from a prosecutor to a preacher? I don't think so, but in every case, God found someone He could work in and through to accomplish His will.

A perfect Savior was the only cure for an imperfect humanity. To be the perfect and acceptable payment for our sins, no human stain, no mortal flesh could be in the spiritual DNA of the Lord Jesus. The fetus is carried in the womb of the mother, but the blood is contributed by the father, and the life of the flesh is in the blood. Learning that she would give birth as a virgin, Mary called Jesus, "My God and my Savior." Mary needed a Savior, too, and she realized it. Mary was precious, but she was a sinner. Despite the teaching of Roman Catholic theology, it was only Jesus, not Mary, who was miraculously conceived. The blood that gave life to our Savior flowed from the very character of God Himself. Whatever it takes to meet your deepest need, our God will surely provide.

CHAPTER 30

Joseph

Matthew 1:18–21, 24–25

1. We Cannot Fully Love Another Until We Fully Love God.

Someone once asked Leonard Bernstein, famed conductor of the New York Philharmonic, which instrument was the most difficult to play. His immediate response was, "the second fiddle." Joseph played an essential part in the Christmas story, but it is easy to lose sight of him with all the magi, shepherds, and angelic choirs. But there he was, chosen by God to live as though he were the biological father of the Savior. The most transcending part of the story of Joseph is his quiet, meditative consideration to make a private dissolution of the engagement. The heartbreak he knew and the humiliation he would face were beyond imagination, yet one priority guided his every thought and act. At all costs, Mary must be protected and suffer no shame. In an era approaching a 60 percent divorce rate, we would do well to study the commitment of one exceptional husband to the girl he would one day wed. The way Joseph acted proved he not only loved Mary, but truly loved Mary's God and his God.

In Revelation 2, Jesus prescribes a remedy for a bride who has lost her love for her groom. Surprisingly, among the ingredients is the striking rebuke: Repent! Repentance is not an athletic, medical, financial, or material term. It is at once biblical, theological, and spiritual. The bride has sinned, and the meaning is clear—she has lost her love for her husband because she has lost her love for Christ. Backsliding is the

115

first way to lose your love for anyone. We can often trace our inability to experience love to the maximum in any relationship to our loss of love for Him. Conversely, Joseph loved Mary devoutly because he loved God even more.

Do you think Mary ever doubted Joseph's love for her? I am guessing there was a not a day that went by that Mary did not remember the pain and the shame that Joseph had endured as the village gossips speculated about the child growing within her. Joseph did more than feel love or talk about love; he demonstrated his love for God and his love for Mary in standing by her side in a profoundly difficult time.

As a teenager, Ruth Bell left her home in China for schooling in Korea, with plans to spend her life as an unmarried missionary to Tibet. Apparently the thought of a husband had entered her mind, but her list of qualifications might have frightened away even the most amazing of men. Listen to what she wrote, "If I marry: He must be so tall that when he is on his knees, he reaches all the way to heaven. His shoulders must be broad enough to bear the burdens of a family. His lips strong enough to smile, firm enough to say no, and tender enough to kiss. His love must be so deep it takes its stand in Christ and so wide it takes the whole world in. He must be active enough to save souls. He must be big enough to be gentle and brave enough to be thoughtful. His arms must be strong enough to carry a little child." Ruth Bell found her man in Billy Graham, a man who loved God passionately. I am not sure Mary ever made a list of what she was looking for in a husband, but God did, and He found that man in Joseph. Because he loved Him so, Joseph knew the richest kind of love for God's very special girl.

2. God Never Forgets Those Who Remember Him.

Have you ever felt forgotten? On several occasions I have seen children accidentally left at church by their parents. The mistake was honest—each parent thought the other had picked the child up from Sunday school or children's church, while neither had. Imagine their embarrassment when they called the church, frantic to make sure someone would wait until they could return and reclaim their special treasure! No one likes being forgotten, and you could not blame Joseph if he felt that way, but there is no record of him ever whining or complaining. All we see is a servant, infinitely patient, willing to make sacrifices, even when it meant moving to Egypt.

Often called "the forgotten man of Christian history," the gentle carpenter was nonetheless eternally remembered by the God he loved so passionately. Of all the men on earth, our Lord chose Joseph to provide an earthly father for His son. Joseph's was the guiding hand that would shape the life of the boy Jesus. His faithful service for Him was not forgotten in the great mind and heart of God. Because Joseph kept God first in his life, our God remembered him and trusted him with the life of His only Son!

While God never forgot Joseph, neither, I'm sure, did Jesus. The lessons learned working side by side with His earthly father would go with Him all the way to the cross. Though Joseph was a borrowed father, Jesus could have never forgotten that of all the men in the world, God chose Joseph.

The story is told of a father and son climbing a mountain. At one point during their ascent, the climb became extremely difficult and dangerous. The father stopped to consider which path to take and heard his son behind him say, "Choose the good path, Dad; I'm coming right behind you." What a great lesson for every dad to remember. Never forget that just as Jesus followed behind Joseph, our children are coming right behind us. And remember that God never forgets those who never forget Him!

3. God Is Always at Work in the Lives of His Children.

One of the amazing aspects of the Christmas story is the number of prophecies that had to be fulfilled. Hundreds of years before, prophets had told of the coming of a Messiah. Their prophecy was not so generic it could be an "anywhere, anytime" kind of prophecy. They did everything but give the names of the earthly parents! Did Joseph and Mary have a choice? I am convinced they did. I believe that either could have sabotaged God's plan, but neither did. Two teenagers met and fell in love, yet each loved the Lord even more than the other. Clearly Mary chose Joseph within the will of God. Her own choice might well have been another. But that would have been the wrong choice. Had she married a lesser man, the likelihood is very small that God would have chosen her to bear His son. Mary could have had a great marriage with another man and never known what might have been. When we make life's choices, the hand of God may be quietly at work. If we seek Him with all our heart, He will grant us the ability to make them wisely.

Pastors have lots of opportunities to make hospital calls and nursing home visits. Over the years I have discovered how much I could learn by simply asking our senior adults to tell me how God has worked in their lives. I have watched faces light up as memories engaged and they began to reminisce about days gone by. Story after story has flowed as they reviewed their lives and pointed out how God's hand had clearly been involved in their journey. And I have discovered you don't have to be old to reflect on God's work in your life. I encourage myself frequently when I recount some of the ways that God has provided for me and for our church.

Recently I boarded a plane in Missouri. The temperature was dropping, and it had snowed all night. The flight was delayed for quite some time, and we finally boarded the plane, only to sit on the runway as the plane was de-iced several times. When we finally took off the visibility was poor, and I remember hoping the pilot could see more outside his window than I could see outside mine. Ten minutes into the flight we broke through the clouds. Suddenly all the darkness was gone, and the sun was shining so brightly no one would have ever dreamed we'd just left the sleet and snow behind. God reminded me that where He works, the sun is always shining. When the angel came calling on Joseph, things looked pretty dark in his world, but God had a plan and would never forget His faithful servant. Wherever you find yourself today, be encouraged. The sun is shining just above the clouds and our God is clearly at work!

Chapter 31

John the Baptist

John 1:27–29

1. Though He May Know Much, No Man Knows It All.

John the Baptist was the first cousin of Jesus. Undoubtedly, they were raised together, played together, and went to synagogue school together. No man knew Jesus better. When John began his earthly ministry, his singular message was, "Repent, for the kingdom of heaven is at hand." John believed Jesus was the long promised earthly Messiah who would overthrow the Roman Empire and establish the kingdom in Israel. He preached what he knew, and he taught what he understood. But then everything changed for John. He came to understand that Jesus was more than an earthly conqueror. He was indeed the eternal sacrifice of God, promised for the sins of the world, who would establish His kingdom in human hearts.

When he prepared the way for Jesus, it was for only an earthly kingdom. When he finished his ministry, he would introduce Him as "the Lamb of God who takes away the sin of the world." John progressively came to understand who Jesus was and what He had really come to do. Beware of thinking we can finally make it on our own, that we have somehow arrived. Those who draw closest to Him and grow most in His likeness see best the length of the road yet to travel.

John's place in the New Testament drama is unique. He is the last of the Old Testament prophets. He is a seer or an illumined one, and a man completely in touch with God. Jesus said of John: "I assure you: Among those born of women no one greater than John the Baptist has appeared" (Matt. 11:11). Now that covers a lot of territory. Noah, Abraham, Moses, Isaiah, Jeremiah, and Elisha all join the list of lesser men when Jesus mentions the name John the Baptist. And yet, there is a peculiar note about him. In John 1:31, John states of Jesus, "I didn't know him."

Only slowly was John convinced of Jesus' divinity. How is it that God grants such greatness to men and still leaves them without vital information? God grants to each a level of wisdom, to each a level of knowledge, to each a measure of faith. Curiously, those levels always leave us lacking. After he had pronounced Jesus "the Lamb of God," John still had questions: "When John heard in prison about what the Messiah was doing, he sent a message by his disciples and asked Him, 'Are you the Coming One, or should we expect someone else?'" (Matt. 11:2–3). God allows us enough, but not too much. *It is His way* to draw us more deeply into a trusting, dependent relationship with Him.

The recent tragedy of the atomic submarine, the USS *Greeneville,* deserves our scrutiny at this point. No ship in the navy is better equipped than an atomic submarine. No crew is better trained, no captain more carefully chosen, and no electronic surveillance equipment more accurate. Yet, despite all of these advantages, there was still a great lack. On a clear day, the crew decided to execute a maneuver that is routine to any submarine. It is called a "main ballast blow." The result of the ballast release is to bring the sub to the surface at a very fast speed. Everything went well until the sub broke the surface and rammed the side of a Japanese fishing vessel, the one hundred ninety-five foot *Ehime Maru.* The accident resulted in loss of life, loss of the *Maru,* loss of position for the captain, and loss of respect for United States Naval operations. How could such a thing happen? The answer lies ultimately in human frailty. According to testimony, the crew and captain followed every prescribed procedure—but they failed to execute their move to the surface in the proper manner.

No one knows everything. None has achieved perfection. Every great person has a dark side, and failure is a stranger to no one. Against this backdrop came Jesus. He was the God-man. He was perfection incarnate and a perfect Savior. It is to Him that all must look, and it is toward Him that John pointed us. It is He who fills up our lack and completes our experience. John's greatness lay in knowing that only in Jesus does all fullness dwell.

2. The Impeccable Character of Our Lord Jesus Will Bear the Most Meticulous Scrutiny.

Listen to the words of Jesus' cousin John the Baptist, who undoubtedly knew Jesus very well:

• He is the One coming after me, whose sandal strap I'm not worthy to untie (John 1:27).
• After me comes a man who has surpassed me, because He existed before me (John 1:30).
• He must increase, but I must decrease (John 3:30).

John the Baptist was beheaded because of what he knew Jesus to be. Men will not die for that in which they do not believe. Scrutinizing the impeccable character of Jesus brought John the Baptist to a willingness to die a martyr's death for Him.

Flavius Josephus, Alfred Edersheim, and Josh McDowell became apologists for the Nazarene whom they originally set out to disprove. And what of Saul of Tarsus, who met him on the road to Damascus? All found themselves captivated by the power of his life. Every spring, activity at jewelry stores increases. With June as our traditional season of matrimony, young men go in search of the perfect ring for the finger of their beloved. Knowing nothing about diamonds, every groom must depend upon counsel from a qualified jeweler. Part of the counsel that every honest jeweler gives is this: "There is no perfect diamond." No matter how perfect it may appear to the naked eye, every stone has a signature flaw. At the cross, every rock on earth cracked, and that apparently includes every diamond.

The greatest among us are subject to imperfection, except one—Jesus, the pearl of great price. Born of a virgin, He was without the imputed sin nature that is Adam's legacy. So powerful was His presence that men were continually confounded by Him. The Pharisees were envious of Him, the demoniac bowed at His feet, the disciples' lives were shaped by Him, and the centurion who crucified Him pronounced Him the Son of God.

What a testimony from him who knew Him well! John the Baptist said that he was not worthy to untie Jesus' sandal strap. John's life and example show that character makes a difference in how we are perceived. When others look closely, it will ultimately be to measure who we really are by our character. Martin Luther King was right on the mark when he said that the worth of a man should not be determined by the color of his skin, but by the content of his character.

Jesus had it all: integrity, discernment, wisdom, righteousness—in summary, perfect character. He is the diamond without a flaw, the pearl of great price, the gold without dross. In short, He is the God-man. The willing sacrifice of John's life backed up John's claim that he was certain Jesus was the Messiah.

3. The Power of Character Outweighs the Force of Circumstances.

Beheaded in prison—why? Because of what he was saying? Because of the glibness of his speech, the biting tone of his rhetoric, the sting of his oratory? No. More. Much more. His lingering influence, the force of his personality, and the haunting effect, not of what he was saying, but of who he was, were so powerful that he would be imprisoned for the sake of the Gospel.

America's bookstores are filled with self-help books promising great achievement through personal power. They counsel us to reach deep inside ourselves and grab onto the dynamo of strength that lies in every human being. Instinctively they know that success is rooted somehow in personality, even if they fail to realize that character is the essential foundation of personality. The key essential to powerful personality is godly character, and godly character comes by God's presence within. John the Baptist was such a man.

In his devotional book *My Utmost for His Highest,* Oswald Chambers writes, "The final stage in the life of faith is character. We have to learn to maintain character up to the last notch revealed in the vision of Jesus Christ." Only by doing so will we impact our world for Christ.

Herod's fear of John the Baptist was a fear of righteous character and a continual reminder of his own unrighteousness. What John *was* frightened Herod far beyond anything he could *do* from his prison cell.

Abraham Lincoln was a man of profound inner strength. When he arrived in Washington most believed him to be a bumbling backwoods lawyer. One of his cabinet members, Salmon Chase, once called him a fool. When a reporter asked him to respond he said, "Well, Mr. Chase is an educated man. If he said that I believe the matter deserves looking into." By the end of our country's Civil War, many had come to believe he had no peer in American history. His character has never been surpassed among succeeding presidents.

After Hurricane Hugo raked across Jamaica in September 1989, destroying crops, homes, and lives, a CNN reporter interviewed a banana farmer about his loss. The farmer responded, "Mon, we've lost our whole crop." The reporter said, "Then I hear you saying you've lost everything." "No," answered the farmer. "I didn't say that; we still have Jesus." That's character, and its power is stronger than any hurricane in the world.

CHAPTER 32
Matthew

Luke 5:27–32

1. Knowing Jesus Christ Requires a 180-Degree Change.

Jesus gave Matthew a simple command. It was not "Follow me *plus*," "Follow me *but*," or "Follow me *if*." It was "Follow me." And Matthew left almost everything for Jesus, right? Wrong. "And he left *all*." What a simple transaction! What a clear and concise picture of conversion! Jesus said, "Follow me," and Matthew followed Him. The person who will follow Jesus must go the same direction that Jesus is going, and that is not the direction anyone walks before knowing the way of the Master.

"He left everything behind." Not tomorrow, not after he'd thought about it, not with qualifications. Right then, without delay—everything and immediately. True discipleship allows for no less.

It is never good enough to simply try to do better. Following Christ begins with an inner transformation that takes us out of the domain of darkness and transfers us into the kingdom of heaven. Living as a disciple of Jesus means nothing less than a radical change of direction. Peter says we should live the rest of the time in the flesh no longer for human desires, but for God's will (1 Pet. 4:2). That is a 180-degree change, and no true discipleship exists without it.

125

2. You Know You're Truly Jesus' Friend When the Right People Are Against You.

Immediately the Pharisees criticized Him. Eating with tax collectors and sinners—unthinkable! The Pharisees are interesting people. I've had to deal with some in my life, and believe me, I'll take a liberal any day. Get an idea, call up the legalists, ask them their opinion, and be sure of one thing— if they don't like the idea, *it's definitely of God.* We can often be most certain that we're in agreement with Jesus if we're in disagreement with the legalists. The legalist looks for what is wrong—grace looks for what is right.

In 1786, young William Carey proposed at a pastors' meeting that they discuss their neglect to obey the Great Commission. This suggestion produced the harsh reply, "Young man, sit down! When God pleases to converse with the heathen He'll do it without consulting you or me!" But William Carey did not sit down. He stood for what he knew was on the heart of God and ushered in the era of modern missions that continues to this very day.

From the very beginning of the Christian life we must be ready to face criticism and opposition. Remember the woman who washed Jesus' feet with bitter tears of repentance and then anointed them with perfume? Her critics couldn't believe this sinner would ever be converted. They didn't think she should have been allowed into the house! In spite of their disapproving groans and grimaces, she washed the Master's feet. Her reward? Jesus said to her, "Your sins are forgiven . . . Your faith has saved you. Go in peace" (Luke 7:48, 50). This is where we must all begin with Jesus and the critics.

From our conversion experience all the way to the end of our earthly life, God calls us to be men and women who will do what is right, regardless of the critics. Take heart from Noah, Caleb, Joshua, Daniel, and a host of saints who have said, "Here I stand!" regardless of what the critics may say. Remember well Jesus' admonition, "Woe to you when people speak well of you, this is the way their forefathers used to treat the false prophets" (Luke 6:26). Rejoice when those who oppose God oppose you. You're on the right path!

3. Those Who Truly Love the Lord Want Everybody to Love Him.

There's nothing like the zeal of a new Christian like Matthew. The first thing Matthew did was to have Jesus over for dinner, and who did he invite? The pastors and staff of the local church? No, he invited his fellow tax collectors. Tax collectors were the most hated people among the Jews. Not only were they exorbitant in their taxation, but they collected from their own people for the benefit of the very Roman empire that was crushing them. And yet they were the ones who stood at the door when Matthew's wife announced, "Guess who's coming to dinner?"

I rejoice when people surrender their lives to the call of God for full-time Christian ministry. But it thrills me even more to see laypeople using that marvelous sphere of influence that preachers seldom penetrate to bring their peers to the Savior. They might tune out the message of a preacher, but they generally listen very readily to a respected professional colleague.

I recall hearing Ralph Neighbor say, "The two most effective tools for evangelism are a fork and a pen." The fork for sharing a meal with your friend who needs Jesus. And the pen for writing a note of encouragement. Much has changed over the last twenty-five years, but the fork and the pen are still amazingly effective tools for reaching the lost. By the way, for those who prefer the keyboard to the pen, make it a personal note, rather than one of those forwarded messages!

The progressive breakdown of the traditional family means that there are increasing numbers of people who long to be invited somewhere for a meal. And though they may not realize it yet, their deepest longing is to meet the One who said, "If anyone hears My voice and opens the door, I will come in to him and have dinner with him, and he with Me" (Rev. 3:20).

You may be a new Christian, or you may have been walking with Christ for many years. In either case, the challenge before us today is the same. Having made that 180-degree change in direction, by the grace of God, you are to stay on course! Don't let the worries of the world and the deceitfulness of riches choke out your passion for the Lord Jesus. There will always be those who scoff at your commitment to follow Christ. Remind yourself every day that the approval of God is much more valuable than the approval of man. Like Matthew, see your network of friends and acquaintances as the net God wants to use to make you a fisher of men and women.

CHAPTER 33

The Demoniac of Gadara

Mark 5:1–13

I like to think of this demon-possessed man as the "Gerasenes gadabout." Chain him and he'd break the chains. Clothe him and he'd tear off his clothes. He loved to run naked, wild, and free. He was, indeed, as a pastor friend entitled a sermon about him, "A Nude Dude in a Rude Mood."

1. The Demonic World Is as Real as the Divine.

This is no fairy tale. It is as real as it is terrible, and it happens every day. As real as are the Father, Son, Holy Spirit, and angels, just as real are the Devil, the Antichrist, false prophets, and demons. One only deceives oneself by scoffing at the reality of Satan and the demonic forces who do his bidding. Deny it at your own hurt. Ignore it at your own loss. Many of your problems have no human answer because they are rooted in the reality and power of the enemy of our souls.

Having said this, let me offer a word of caution: You may just as easily get caught up in the opposite, a fantasy world that suggests that every normal problem confronting us is a demonic manifestation. Obsession with the demonic is equally as erroneous as denial of it.

You cannot read the Bible without seeing the presence of Satan from beginning to end. He was in the Garden of Eden. He brought disaster into Job's life. A demonic spirit afflicted King Saul. (Satan moved King David to sin against God by counting his victorious army.) The answer to Daniel's prayer was delayed because a demonic spirit fought against Gabriel and Michael. Throughout His ministry on earth, Jesus was constantly rebuking and casting out demons. The pattern continued with the apostles in the Book of Acts. Thankfully, the closing chapters of Revelation tell of Satan's final defeat. Until then, Peter says, "Be sober! Be on the alert! Your adversary the Devil is prowling around like a roaring lion, looking for anyone he can devour. Resist him, firm in the faith" (1 Pet. 5:8–9). James exhorts us, "Therefore, submit to God. But resist the Devil, and he will flee from you" (James 4:7).

In Luke 11:14–26, Jesus responded to the Pharisees' accusation that He was casting out demons by the power of Satan. Jesus clearly states that there are two kingdoms: the kingdom of Satan and the kingdom of God. Both kingdoms require unity to function properly, for "every kingdom divided against itself is headed for destruction."

He says, "Anyone who is not with Me is against Me, and anyone who does not gather with Me scatters." He goes even further to indicate that there may be demonic consequences for those who attempt neutrality. Jesus tells of a man from whom a demon had departed. The man enjoys temporary relief, but soon the demon returns to his former residence. Jesus says, "And returning, it finds the house swept and put in order. Then it goes and brings seven other spirits more evil than itself, and they enter and settle down there. As a result, that man's last condition is worse than the first." I will not try to answer the many questions this passage raises, but suffice it to say, if your life is not indwelt by the Spirit of Christ, you are an open target for the enemy. There is no neutral ground!

It is not uncommon to hear people refer to their bad habits or emotional hang-ups as "my demons." What do you think the Gerasene demoniac would say about that expression if he were here today? Likely, something like this: "Man, don't even talk to me about having demons! But if you've got one, I know who can set you free!"

2. Without God, Even the Strongest Are Helpless before Satan.

Men had forged chains of iron. Men had done all they could to bind the raging forces that drove the demoniac of Gerasa, but he snapped the shackles apart like paper ribbons at a child's birthday party. And how so? By his own human power? No. As Samson only did what he did by God's power, the demoniac only did what he did by Satan's power. The greatest physician, pharmacist, psychologist, or psychiatrist is helpless without the power of Christ before the power of Satan.

We do ourselves a grave disservice to flippantly sing, "If the Devil doesn't like it he can sit on a tack." There are stern warnings in Scripture against making light of the powers of the enemy. There are serious consequences for those who speak abusively against what they do not understand. Satan's kingdom is no laughing matter.

Almost every culture has shamans, witch doctors, or exorcists who specialize in dealing with the supernatural. Even in secular, scientific America, there is an increasing interest in learning how to deal with spirits and powers beyond ourselves. A constant stream of movies, television programs, and books deals with the supernatural. It is vital that we approach the supernatural very carefully and from a biblical perspective.

In Acts 19, we find recorded a humorous yet sobering event involving some Jewish exorcists. They had observed how effective Paul was at casting out demons, so they decided to try it. Foolishly, they commanded the demons to come out "by the Jesus whom Paul preaches." But Scripture says, to their chagrin, "The evil spirit answered them, 'Jesus I know, and Paul I recognize, but who are you?' Then the man who had the evil spirit leaped on them, overpowered them all, and ran out of that house naked and wounded." You may not have noticed, but Satan seems to have a thing about nudity!

Without a personal relationship with God, we are helpless before Satan! "Who are you?" was the question the demon asked. What would your answer have been? The Jewish exorcists evidently were dumbfounded. They didn't know who they were. They just knew they'd better run for it! Apart from a blood covenant relationship with almighty God, we, too, may be victims of Satan. Though few may actually be demon possessed, Scripture says of those who do not have a faith relationship with Christ that the Devil has taken them captive to do his will. Jesus said to the unbelieving Jews, "You are of your father the Devil, and you want to carry out your father's desires" (John 8:44).

It is a basic principle of the Christian life that we must first acknowledge our weakness and inability to deal with the task at hand. Until we admit we are helpless and hopelessly lost, we are not candidates for salvation. This principle also holds true for every subsequent step in the Christian life in the battle against Satan. The children's song says it profoundly, "I am weak, but He is strong. Yes, Jesus loves me!"

3. The Power of Jesus Is the Only Force Greater than the Power of Satan.

Having stated the fact of Satan's power, let's move on to the good news! In the passage I mentioned earlier (Luke 11:14–26), Jesus described Himself as "one stronger" than the Devil. In fact, in Luke 11:20, Jesus said He cast out demons "by the finger of God." That's all it takes! Just the finger of God! It is vital that we don't view the conflict between God and Satan as dualism. It's not the good side fighting against the dark side. There is no comparison between the power of God and the power of the Devil. The legion of demons in the demoniac begged Jesus for permission to go into the herd of swine. They knew they were whipped! Jesus has a position of power and authority far above all principality, and power, and might, and dominion, and every name that is named, not only in this world, but in that which is to come! The Devil and his angels shudder and cringe at the name of Jesus. A word from His mouth or a flick of His finger is all it takes for Jesus to set the prisoner free from Satan's power.

Jesus said, "If the Son sets you free, you really will be free" (John 8:36). Isaiah 61:1 prophesies that our Lord has come "to proclaim freedom for the captives and release from darkness for the prisoner." Satan has the power of death. The forces of sin, hell and the grave are at his disposal. His strongholds in us can make life an endless nightmare, a living hell from which death would be a release. First John 3:8 says, "The Son of God was revealed for this purpose: to destroy the Devil's works." At the cross, Jesus grappled with all the forces and power of Satan, crying, "It is finished!" He ascended from the grave with the keys to hell swinging at his belt, saying, "I am the resurrection and the life."

Jesus constantly spoke of the coming of the kingdom of God. The clear implication is that the kingdom of Satan was being conquered and replaced by the kingdom of Jesus. The stumbling block for the Jews was that Jesus' first coming was not in power and great glory, crushing Satan and the Roman Empire with an iron rod. Be assured—the time is drawing near when Jesus will come as a mighty conqueror seated on a white horse (Rev. 19:11, 15–16; 20:10).

Isaiah 61:1 prophesies that our Lord has come "to proclaim freedom for the captives and release from darkness for the prisoner."

We live in an age between the first coming and the second coming of Christ. The kingdom has arrived, but contrary to the Jews' expectations, it came quietly and unobtrusively and is only in our hearts. At His second coming however, the Lord Jesus will usher in His glorious kingdom that will last forever!

Have you ever seen a huge building demolished on TV? That's what God is doing to the kingdom of Satan. He has strategically placed His explosives in the structure of the demonic realm. At the Resurrection He activated the igniter. Satan's kingdom is crumbling and crashing down! It's happening in slow motion at this time, but Satan's doom is sealed. He and all his demons can do nothing to avoid defeat. But the moment of final victory when the demolition will speed up to real time is yet to come. We await the awesome return of Jesus. Then the kingdom of Satan and all the kingdoms of this world will be shattered to nothing but dust (Dan. 2:34–35, 44–45). The demolition will be complete! You can see why John ends the book of Revelation with the statement, "Amen. Come, Lord Jesus!"

The demoniac of Gerasa was held hostage in the dungeon of Satan's kingdom. But, oh, that wonderful day when Jesus set foot on his shore! He delivered the demoniac from the legion of demons that had caused violence, insanity, masochism, and nudity to dominate his life. He was free indeed! And Jesus told him, "Go back home to your own people, and report to them how much the Lord has done for you and how he has had mercy on you (Mark 5:19)." The demoniac of Gerasa became the evangelist of Gerasa! The most hopeless case of them all was settled by just a few powerful words from the lips of the Savior, with whom nothing shall be impossible.

The story of the demoniac of Gerasa has a great ending. How about your story? God knows what you're going through today. And He is here. Ready to set you free. Come to Him. Declare today with David, "The LORD is the stronghold of my life—of whom shall I be afraid?" (Ps. 27:1).

CHAPTER 34

Peter

Matthew 26:57–58, 69–74

1. The Greater the Distance from Jesus, the Greater the Risk.

When Simon Peter got away from Jesus, he usually found himself in trouble. His spiritual life had been a roller coaster, to say the least. For three years the highs had been higher than high, but now the lows could hardly be lower.

"Meanwhile, Peter was following Him at a distance." What a sad commentary on the man who had boasted, "Even if everyone falls because of you, I will never fall!" (Matt. 26:33). We do well to take heed when we think we stand, lest we fall. The servant is certainly not greater than his Lord, and our Lord Jesus made a massive effort to be close to the Father in times of impending trial and temptation. For forty days in the wilderness, He fasted and prayed before His great confrontation with the wicked one. In John 17:19, He committed Himself afresh to His Father prior to Gethsemane. He prayed all night before His arrest and trial. The example of Christ should have been a model for Peter and certainly is for us.

Bumper stickers often warn us not to follow too closely. But Jesus says just the opposite—He invites us to come close. We only fool ourselves if we think we can live at a distance from Him and call on Him in our emergencies. In many ways Peter was an embarrassment not only to himself, but certainly to the entire apostolic band, and even to the Christian world. It's only a matter of time until serious trouble befalls the believer who chooses to live his life as a distant follower of the Lord.

I love the story about the toddler whose mother had just tucked him into bed. She went downstairs and was cleaning the kitchen when she heard a thud and then a cry. Racing upstairs, she found her little boy on the floor, where he had fallen out of bed. When she asked what had happened, he replied, "I guess I fell asleep too close to where I got in!" How often does that happen in the believer's life? We walk with Christ, but at what we think is a comfortable distance. God invites us to come close.

2. Delay in Decision Hardens the Heart.

Waiting can be very valuable, but not when it comes to standing for the truth. Three times Peter was accused of being a disciple as his Lord endured the humiliation of a trial. The first time he denied he knew Him. The second, he denied Him with an oath. The third time he cursed as he denied his Lord. Peter dug the hole deeper and deeper, and each time his heart grew harder and his voice louder. Statistics used to tell us that 95 percent of all the people who make decisions for Christ do so before their eighteenth birthday. Today they are saying the age has dropped to thirteen. Is that an accident? I don't think so. The earlier in life a person can make a commitment to Christ, the better. Years of heartache and pain can be avoided when those tender hearts accept the Good News of Christ. Churches and ministries need to channel resources into people and programs that are committed to reaching the children and youth of our world. They can make no greater investment.

We postpone many decisions because we erroneously assume that we'll make the decision more easily if we wait awhile. In fact, delay makes it harder. God's grace was greater than Satan's deceptions, so that, eventually, Peter realized the depth of God's love and boldly proclaimed it to everyone. But how much embarrassment could the big fisherman have saved himself had he simply told the truth from the beginning, answering yes when asked, "Are you one of His?"

3. He Deceives Himself Who Seeks the Benefits of Discipleship Without the Relationship.

Far greater than the risk of keeping Christ at a distance is the possibility we may not know Him at all. Jesus says, "If you continue in my Word, you really are my disciples" (John 8:31). The book of James makes it clear that phony faith talks a good game, but saving faith endures to the end. Enduring does not contribute to one's salvation; it validates it.

Annual Easter worshipers need to closely examine their profession of faith in Christ. Far more likely than the possibility of losing one's salvation is the likelihood that distant disciples only reveal themselves for what they are—hypocrites who never really had salvation in the first place. Am I raising the question of Peter's salvation at this point in his life? Indeed, I am. Certainly one must question the faith of a man who would fight to keep Jesus from the very cross that would save his soul. Disciples are learners, and the word "disciple" means "to seek after truth." One does not color too far outside the lines in questioning whether any of the disciples had really understood the whole story and come to salvation before they saw the resurrected Christ.

Three times Jesus asked Peter, "Do you love me?" Surely our Lord intended for Peter to carefully search his heart. Jesus wanted Peter to be sure. We would be wise to do no less.

Chapter 35

Andrew

John 1:37–42

1. Reconciling Men to God Is the Highest Work of the Redeemed.

Little is known of Andrew, for he appears as just one of the twelve in Matthew and Luke. But three times Andrew stands alone, clearly marking his own identity apart from the apostolic band. In each of the three, he is bringing someone to Jesus. He first brought Simon, his brother, whom the Lord named Peter. He brought the lad with the loaves and fishes to Jesus, as well as the Greeks who came with that mighty request, "Sirs, we would see Jesus." No president who has ever sat or king who has ever reigned has approached the eternal importance of the most humble, insignificant believer who faithfully brings men and women to the Lord Jesus.

Andrew's calling was simple, as recorded in Matthew 4:19: "Follow Me, and I will make you fishers of men!" Jesus called to him in language that the professional fisherman understood. Yet the challenge was beyond his capacity to perform alone. He realized that he couldn't fish for men on his own (Acts 1:8).

Jesus offered Andrew a challenge as a condition of his discipleship. This command/promise format meant that if he wasn't following, he wouldn't be fishing. Conversely, if we're not fishing, we're not following as Christ intended. All three times Andrew "makes the Book," he is accomplishing the greatest task of all—bringing someone to the Master.

2. Inferiority Complexes Need Not Keep Us from Being Superior People.

He is so often mentioned in passing as "Andrew, Simon Peter's brother" that one must wonder if he did not develop an inferiority complex. If anyone had reason to do so, Andrew did. A psychiatrist told his client, "I've got some good news for you and some bad. I've determined that you do not have an inferiority complex after all. You really are inferior." And the fact is, most of us are if we compare ourselves to others. But Jesus would have us keep our eyes on Him who lifts the downcast and encourages the heart of the insecure. For we can do superior work for Him as we come to understand that we become mature and Christlike by no effort of our own, but by the life of Him who lives within.

A defining moment for Andrew's trust occurred during the storm on the Sea of Galilee, as recorded in Mark 4:35–41: "Let's cross over to the other side of the lake." Jesus clearly promised the disciples they were going to the other side. But in the middle of the storm, they doubted His Word. In fact, they marveled at His power, clearly not understanding who He was. The key to any Christian's peace in the midst of a storm comes through walking by faith and not by sight. God gives us hundreds of specific promises to which to cling. A Christian will not doubt in the darkness what he or she learns in the light. Superior people are just inferior people who have learned to trust the promises of God.

This was a powerful storm. Matthew 8:24 uses the Greek word *seismos,* leading us to picture the force of an earthquake. Mark gives a vivid eyewitness account of the waves breaking over the gunwales into the boat, of the boat taking on water, and a situation growing far beyond the disciples' ability to manage! Only Jesus could do that, and manage it He did.

For Andrew and the others, Jesus' ability to calm the seas caused a major paradigm shift. Perhaps at this very moment, Andrew came to the end of his ability and learned to rely on the Lord's. Perhaps in some way, he stepped out of Peter's shadow in order to follow in Christ's. In that moment Andrew became God's man and in so doing, perhaps for the first time in his life, became his own man as well.

3. The Best Decisions Are Those That Are Patiently and Thoughtfully Made.

In John 1:35–39 we find Andrew, a serious student of the things of God, seeking to know even more about Jesus. Andrew had learned all that John the Baptist could teach him, and stood tall alongside the great prophet as his disciple. When John moved from introducing Jesus as an earthly Messiah whom the Jews believed would overthrow the Roman empire, to the Lamb of God who would set up a kingdom within peoples' hearts, Andrew wanted to know more. He would make a serious and studied decision. His question to Jesus, "Where are you staying?" is not a casual one. Andrew wanted to spend the night with Jesus and learn more about His background. "Who are you? Where did you come from? Where do you live?" he would ask.

The power of the Gospel is such that millions who hear it for the first time believe. When I preached in Russia in 1992, forty-six hundred of the six thousand in attendance virtually ran down the aisles to trust Jesus Christ as their Savior. Just as real, however, is the decision of those who think deeply, giving long and serious consideration to the claims of Christ. Those who take time to know Him will come to love Him completely. Few have not heard the name of Alfred Edersheim, the brilliant Jewish historian who wrote *The Life and Times of Jesus the Messiah.* But how many know that Rabbi Edersheim set out in his book to disprove Jesus was the Messiah He claimed to be? His thoughtful study ultimately led him to pronounce Jesus Christ as Lord. Today his work stands as one of the classical apologetic defenses of the Savior.

CHAPTER 36

Mary Magdalene

Luke 8:1–2; Mark 16:1; John 20:15–16

1. Our Lord Never Tires of the Praises of His People.

Magdala was a city known exclusively for its one and only business—prostitution! The nickname term "Mary the Magdalene" was a synonym for "Mary the prostitute." It was common to call someone by the name of their city. Judas Iscariot was Judas of "Cariot"—incidentally, the hometown of Sirhan Sirhan, who assassinated Robert Kennedy; Saul was "of Tarsus," and our Lord was "Jesus of Nazareth." With Mary the Magdalene, however, the name meant much more than just where she was from—it revealed what she was. At the empty tomb Jesus would call her by the sweetest name she would ever hear: "Mary," plain and simple.

She who had been forgiven so much could never stop showering her gratitude on the Lord Jesus. Dr. Luke writes of her, "She was a sinner." He adds that seven demons had been cast out of her life. Is there any question that at least one of those was the demon of lust? And can there be any question that the woman who broke the alabaster box and washed His feet with her tears was Mary Magdalene? Of no other Mary in the New Testament, and there are several, does a gospel writer specifically state, while leaving her unnamed, "Who was a sinner." Mary Magdalene's exuberance of worship was the natural result of the gratitude for the massive spiritual healing that had taken place in her life. Those of us who are older have lived lives that have known little of drugs and the

141

occult, let alone immorality and addiction, to the degree of our young people today. Could their exuberance of worship, which so often disturbs older believers, be related to the greater depth of sin from which they have come?

2. To Whom Much Is Given, Much Is Expected.

Mary Magdalene's exuberance of appreciation for the transforming power of Jesus' touch was not exclusively expressed in her occasional outbursts of jubilant worship, but in her consistent service to the Master. Luke 8:2 introduces us to a band of faithful women who followed Jesus and the disciples to minister to their every need. Luke writes they did this out of their own personal wealth. Eight such appearances of this group of faithful women are recorded in the gospels, and in each Mary Magdalene is first in the list of names. We are not surprised to find that she who had been a slave of Satan gladly spent her life working so hard for her new Master. And can we do less?

An anonymous author gave the following stark image:

If God granted you 70 years of life, you would spend:

- 23 years sleeping
- 14 years working
- 8 years at the television
- 8 years in amusement
- 6 years eating
- 4 years in transportation
- 4 years in conversation
- 1 year reading
- 1 year in education

If you went to church every Sunday and stayed until the last hymn and prayed five minutes morning and night, you would be giving God five months of your life. Five months out of 70 years? To whom much is given, much indeed is required.

3. God Saves the Best for Those Who Give Him Their Best.

Someone may well have said to Joseph of Arimathaea, "That was such a beautiful, costly, hand-hewn tomb. Why did you not give it to someone else to be interred in?" Wouldn't this have been a wonderful answer? "Oh, He only needed it for the weekend."

At least a dozen post-Resurrection appearances of Christ are recorded. In order to ensure that everyone had seen Him alive, Jesus appeared to virtually every segment of society, once to a gathering of more than five hundred persons. And to whom would go the honor of the first appearance of the risen Christ? None other than Mary Magdalene. Read again the account of the Resurrection in Matthew 28. It is Mary Magdalene who sees Him first. And He called her, not Mary Magdalene, or Mary the Harlot, but simply "Mary." She was, in His eyes, no longer Mary the Magdalene, just Mary the child of God, who makes all things new, and made her new indeed.

There are three aspects from John 20:11–18 worth noting about Jesus' death and resurrection and their effects on Mary Magdalene:

- *Remorse*—"But Mary stood outside facing the tomb, crying." Mary's request to take Him away reveals her desire to claim the body and pay her final respects. In her mind, He was dead, never to be seen alive again.
- *Recognition*—Turning around, she said to Him in Hebrew, *"Rabboni!"* Many theories have been advanced for the failure of Jesus' disciples to immediately recognize Him. The disciples on the road to Emmaus finally do so when He breaks bread, but Mary does not recognize him until she hears the sweet sound of her own name.
- *Release*—"Don't cling to me." Jesus was not forbidding Mary to touch Him. In fact, He invited Thomas to do so. His instructions had to do with His purpose: He had an assignment, a mission for Mary. Just as the Gerasene demoniac was prohibited from staying with Jesus, but

rather sent forth to share the news, so was Mary to go and tell others the Good News. As Christians, we must be careful not to cling to Jesus while ignoring our mission.

Praise and worship that does not translate into personal evangelism is worship not rooted in spirit and in truth. Jesus both empowers us and releases us to go forth bearing the Good News! After all her sad and sorrowful days, the woman so many loathed became the woman Jesus loved. From Mary Magdalene to Mary, there beamed a million light years of grace. It is often a long wait, but well worth the time for those who are touched by the Master's hand.

CHAPTER 37

Martha

Luke 10:38–42

1. True Service to God Consists of More Than Mere Activity.

Martha was in the kitchen, wondering what she had gotten herself into. She was busy preparing a great meal and the aroma filled the house. As she cooked, Jesus was speaking, about what we do not know, but we do know that her sister, Mary, was sitting at Jesus' feet, intently listening. Perhaps Martha's blood pressure was like one of those pots on the fire—warming up, then simmering, and finally boiling. Martha worked herself into a frenzy, her plate full in more ways than one. How could it be fair for her to slave over a hot oven while her sister was loafing? Finally, she could take it no longer and marched in to speak, not to Mary, but to Jesus.

Martha may well be the most underrated woman in the New Testament. She truly loved the Lord, or else she never would have invited Him into her home and set about to prepare Him a wonderful meal. She was an industrious and hospitable woman but, unfortunately, a good deal of what she was doing was for Martha, as well as for the Lord. I imagine that Martha thought she was going to get the support of Jesus in this situation. Instead, Jesus says, "Martha, Martha, you are worried and upset about many things, but only one thing is necessary. Mary has made the right choice, and it will not be taken away from her." Martha reminds each of us that our strengths can become our weaknesses when they are carried to extremes. With all her good qualities, Martha lacked sensitivity. She was not sensitive to what a special time this was in the life of her sister, and could have been for her.

Few are more tempted at this point than pastors. Trying to build their churches larger and larger and dealing with the pressures of meetings, deadlines, conferences, and counseling can become substitutes for genuine spirituality. Certainly there are priorities in life and in ministry. If the pastorate is anything, it is an endless pressure to choose between the good and the best. But we deceive ourselves when we exchange quiet time and solitude with God for endless busy activities.

Perhaps saddest of all is to never learn that when we put first priority on our time alone with Him, our day is actually less hectic, for He goes before us to organize our day and smooth our way. Give Him ten minutes in the morning and it will take fourteen hours to do your day's work. Give Him an hour and you may accomplish the same in eight.

2. Time with God Is the Only Absolute Imperative in Life.

Jesus said, "Mary, you are disturbed and working on many projects, but only one thing is necessary, and that is to do what Martha is doing . . . hearing my Word, listening to my voice, learning at my feet." What a statement! That is all you really need. To hear His voice and know His Word will teach us His will, make us effective, lead us to right decisions, and positively affect everything in our lives. Remember what Jesus said in Matthew 6:33: "But seek first the kingdom of God and His righteousness, and all these things will be provided for you." Everything else can be let go, delayed, or pushed into distant second place in your life, but miss the priority to be with Him in the morning, and nothing else will be truly successful at all.

Worship is always more important than worry and work. Intellectually we can agree with that statement, but is it reflective of the way we really live? Jesus knew that His time was short. He was on His way to Jerusalem to be crucified, and I'm guessing that food was not a high priority during those hours before he began his final trials. Unfortunately,

I'm afraid that worship is not a high priority in many lives today. I am not talking just about corporate worship, but private worship, as well. Mary was not in the synagogue, and she was not in a public worship service. She was in the privacy of her own home, sitting at the feet of Jesus.

Worry is a draining emotion and occurs in people of all temperaments and personality types. Probably nothing is quite as damaging to worship as worry, for worry takes our eyes off Christ and puts them on ourselves and our problems. It says to God, "I'm not sure You can handle this situation, so I'm going to carry it around and wrestle with it." What about you? Are you worried about something? Has it begun to affect both your private and your public worship? Give that worry over to God and enjoy some serious time resting in His wonderful presence.

3. Our Reward Is a Relationship, Not a Religion.

We do not serve Christ in order to get a paycheck. Some of us have the good fortune of having our material needs met by being employed in ministry. But even in our case, if we are doing it for a paycheck we won't last very long. Mary enjoyed her reward, which was personal friendship with Jesus. She knew that the best way to grow a relationship is to spend time together, and she was doing just that. Mary could have been the one to get angry, instead of Martha. The sister on the floor could have resented the sister at the sink. Mary could have grabbed Jesus by the hand and taken Him into the kitchen, complaining, "Why don't you tell Martha to quit being so productive and to take some time to be reflective. Jesus, don't You think she should be a little more like me?"

Most of us have full plates, literally and figuratively. They may be full of work or worry, strengths that have become weaknesses. Jesus wants you to do more than endure life. He wants you to enjoy the relationship and not suffer through the burden of a religion. As He was there for Martha and Mary, He is there for you and me. All we have to do is take serious time to get to know Him.

CHAPTER 38

The Woman with the Issue of Blood

Luke 8:42–48

1. Our Lord Is Never Too Busy for Us.

Jesus was on the way to an important mission. Jairus had asked Him to come to his home and heal his very sick daughter. What a priority! How focused our Lord must have been! A precious young life hung in the balance, and many who followed Him would see the miracle and believe. An influential father would likely become a convert. And yet He stopped in the middle of a pressing crowd of people and responded to the urgent matter immediately before Him, taking time for a woman who had suffered for twelve long years. Her problem was difficult for a woman in any era, but particularly difficult in that day. As a Jewish woman, nothing could be worse, and it affected every area of her life. She was physically exhausted, socially ostracized, and ceremonially unclean when she came in search of Jesus. But she was not disappointed; Jesus always has time for seekers. What an example for all who would call themselves ministers of the Gospel!

How unlike many pastors and other Christian leaders, who appear to be highly organized and programmed *executives first, and shepherds of the flock only at a distant second.* Let us always remember that people are never an interruption to our ministry. They *are* our ministry. If you are too busy to meet the needs of a hurting congregation when they need you, you are too busy to be a pastor. Our Lord was never that busy, and the servant is not greater than his Lord, nor is his schedule ever more important or crowded. I'm convinced when our public ministry is over, our private ministry will be most remembered. Sermons and ceremonies are important at the time, but it is those moments spent in an intensive care waiting room or those prayers prayed in a funeral home that have the most lasting impact. Who needs some of your love and your time today?

2. Persistent Faith Moves the Hand of God.

She would not be denied. She had pursued healing at the hands of the noted physicians of her day. Over twelve long years she had exhausted her patience, her possibilities of healing, and her financial substance. The Talmud offered eleven cures for her condition, and no doubt she had tried them all. Some were legitimate treatments and others but hollow superstitions, such as carrying the ashes of an ostrich egg in a linen cloth. Financial strain on top of physical pain added insult to injury, and yet she would press on, following Jesus for perhaps a very long time. The crowds were large, and it was most difficult to get close to Him. But day after day she was there, inching closer and closer, until at last she could touch Him. Onward through the crowd, where she could straighten her arm, extend her fingers and finally, on her knees, reach past the ankles of others and barely touch the hem of His garment.

This incident in the life of Jesus is a living testimonial to His promise to His own: "Ask and ye shall receive, seek and ye shall find, knock and it shall be opened unto you. For him that asketh receiveth. He that seeketh findeth, and to him that knocketh it shall be opened" (Luke 11:9–10 KJV). Each of these verbs come from tenses in the Greek language that indicate persistence. Keep on knocking. Keep on asking. Keep on seeking. Never let up. Our Lord is responsive to the importunity of those who long for His miraculous touch.

Do you realize how risky this was for her? In order to touch Him, she had to first touch other people, unclean people, diseased people, hoping somehow to steal a miracle. But persistent faith is a conviction that God can work a miracle and a hope that He will work one for you. Faith is believing God is real and God is good. Sometimes we see faith as far too mystical. But faith is a choice. Faith is not believing God can do what you ask, it is choosing to believe He will. God always honors radical, risk-taking faith. This woman went out on a limb, but God didn't leave her there. He never does!

3. God Is Very Sensitive to the Needs of His Children.

Scripture reminds us we are not heard for our much speaking. The prophets of Baal wailed and cried to no avail. Our high priest is not untouched by the feeling of our infirmities. Our God is a sensitive God, a Man of Sorrows, a weeping Savior who grieves not simply over our sins, but over our deepest hurts and most desperate needs. She did not grab Him, yell at Him or embrace Him. She barely touched Him, and yet immediately power and healing that cost Him dearly flowed from His life into hers and she was whole. He was instantly aware that life had gone from Him. Our Lord does not meet our needs without deep sacrifice. His love and healing flow from the very depth of His soul. He knows when I hurt, and He really cares. And it is not without great price that His virtue becomes ours. The hymn writer said it so well, "Does Jesus Care?" Indeed He does, and He never changes.

Two things happened in this story that did not happen anywhere else in the Bible. First, Jesus apparently healed before He even knew it. It is almost as if God circumvented the normal process of healing, as power flowed out of Jesus instantaneously. Second, Jesus called her "Daughter." When do you think was the last time that she received that kind of affection? Leo Tolstoy, the great Russian writer, tells of walking down the street and passing a beggar. He reached into his pocket to give him some money, but his pocket was empty.

Tolstoy turned to the man and said, "I am sorry, my brother, but I have nothing to give." The beggar brightened and said, "You have given me more than I asked. You have called me 'brother.'"

Tradition holds that this woman never forgot Jesus, and that she followed Him all the way to Calvary and was there when He hung on the cross. Yes, He cares. He really cares!

CHAPTER 39

The Woman at the Well

John 4:4, 7, 10, 16–24

1. Our Savior's Love Reaches to All People.

Our text reveals a vital imperative: Jesus "had to travel through Samaria." Our Lord recognized no human barriers between members of His creation. Jesus came to bring us together and proves it again by His choice to enter the land of Jewish outcasts. The Pharisees required that no Jewish man ever speak to a woman on the street, much less a Samaritan woman. They considered such an act to be anathema, but the loving heart of Jesus was unrestrained.

Jesus' disciples were probably humiliated at His choice to walk upon Samaritan soil. They had much to learn about the heart of the Father. The Holy Spirit would continue to whittle away at their prejudices, until some of these very men would one day see hundreds of Samaritans come into the kingdom at the preaching of Philip.

What boundaries have been superficially erected within your heart? Is it a social class or national origin or skin color that blocks your heart from loving as Jesus did? Our Lord would open our hearts as He did the hearts of His disciples to see the fields white unto harvest, among them some of the very ones we have rejected. Perhaps the Father has designated you to be the harvester.

2. Meeting a Person at Their Point of Need Is the Key to Leading Them to God.

Jesus beautifully demonstrates how to love another into the kingdom with His approach to this woman left tattered and torn by life. He begins by finding a common ground through a brief exchange about water from a well. Masterfully, Jesus draws a parallel between physical water and spiritual refreshment. What an example He has provided in moving from the natural to the supernatural! He touched a chord in her heart as He spoke of eternal satisfaction. Who would not be interested in knowing how to live forever? Jesus stirred her interest and brought her to the very core of her emptiness.

A sick soul cannot be healed without getting to the root of the problem. With tenderness and precision, He patiently shines a spotlight on the inner recesses of the stain in her heart. None can be saved who have yet to understand they are lost. To confront a person about sin is uncomfortable, to say the least. Yet Jesus did so with such love and kindness, that instead of retreating, she was drawn to this stranger.

The woman at the well did what most would in such a moment. Attempting to shift the focus, she grabbed from midair one of the spiritual controversies of the day and threw it upon the pathway of the conversation. She wanted to talk about everything but her sin, but Jesus politely returned her to the matter of her heart and her relationship with the Father.

Jesus was patient. He was not obtrusive or harsh with her, but He was firm. The issue of her sin needed to be brought to the surface before the warm light of His forgiveness could shine in her heart. We come to Him not on our terms, but on His.

3. The True Worship of God Is Never in Form but in Substance.

The woman's question about the correct place in which to worship masked her underlying problem, and one which remains with us today. The physical aspects of worship, whether true worship be here on Mount Gerizim or there in Jerusalem, is never the issue. Jesus made it clear that worship is not about tents or cathedrals, guitars or organs, contemporary music or traditional. Those who needlessly perpetuate arguments about the forms of worship completely miss the point. Jesus said true worship is a matter of the heart, and the only elements of importance are sincerity of spirit and uncompromising devotion to biblical truth.

Our Father inhabits the praise of those whose hearts are fully devoted to Him, and He places an extremely high premium on the sincerity of the worshiper. To offer the Lord our best in skill and refinement is analogous to offering the best of our flock to Him. Such a gift should not be taken, however, as the sum total of all He desires. Samuel reminds us that our God does not desire sacrifice if we do not also give Him our obedience and love. This was the point Jesus made to the woman that day. Our Heavenly Father desires from us not a ritual, but a relationship that is based on truth and comes from a spirit of genuine devotion and sincerity.

CHAPTER 40

The Woman Taken in Adultery

John 8:1–11

1. The Pharisee Goes to Any Length to Look Better Than Others.

These men may well be the biggest hypocrites in the Bible. One does not commit adultery in the open.

How did those who brought this poor woman to Jesus know where to find her? Clearly they knew who she was and where she was. And, by the way, where was her partner? Were the Pharisees protecting one of their own? Why did they single out only the woman? The unnamed man was as guilty as she.

In reality, their concern was not only to punish the woman, but to embarrass the Savior and to make themselves look good. The Pharisee will stay up all night thinking of ways to do that. Matthew says this incident happened early in the morning. Perhaps they had set the trap the night before and had planned the plot to expose her at just the right time. Beware of the person with the constant obsession to "one up" everybody else. That person is probably covering more than you know.

2. No One Has the Right to Judge Another.

Jesus' statement, "The one without sin among you should be the first to throw a stone at her," is a classic. If one thing is constant about Jesus' manner of dealing with sin, it is that He is always harder on those who condemn sinners than the sinners themselves. He said, "I have not come to call the righteous, but sinners to repentance" (Luke 5:32). He is referring, of course, to the self-righteous. They that think themselves whole do not think they need a physician. More harm has been done to the Christian faith through the years by self-righteous legalists than by all the liberals in the world. The one who constantly judges others only reveals a beam in the accuser's own eye much larger than the alleged speck in the eye of another.

Looking at Jesus' words about obeying rules, we need to stop a moment to note four important points about Jewish law:

- *Definition* of the Law (verse 17)—Sources for Jewish laws were: the Ten Commandments, the Pentateuch, (the first five books of the Bible), the Torah (oral interpretation of the Scribal law), and the Old Testament, usually referenced as the "law and the prophets."
- *Duration* of the Law (verse 18)—Jesus, who was accused of being a law breaker (Matt. 5:17; 12:1–14), declares that the smallest letter of the law is set in stone until all is fulfilled.
- *Deference* to the Law (verse 19)—Jesus' words seem to the scribes and the Pharisees to be at odds with His actions in Matthew 12. The reason was because these "teachers of the Law" had elevated their own commentary and interpretation to the status of law itself.
- *Demands* of the Law (verse 20)—When the people heard Jesus exhort them to exceed the righteousness of the scribes and Pharisees, they must have been amazed. Judging others was out. Self-judgment was in. Pride was out. Humility was in, and they were as guilty as the woman accused. We must turn the other cheek, give our cloak freely, and go the second mile. And, above all, we must not focus on a speck in someone else's eye, while we do not notice the beam in our own.

3. Where There Is No Cessation of Sin, There Is No Forgiveness of Sin.

Mixed with Jesus' tenderness with the woman is the unbending, unalterable quality of forgiveness. Jesus' words, "Neither do I condemn you," were inseparably linked to, "Go, and from now on do not sin any more." The command to stop sinning is the condition of the forgiveness of sin. In the model prayer, Jesus taught us to forgive those who sin against us, but quickly added, "For if you do not forgive others, neither will your father in heaven forgive you."

The best definition of repentance is the simple four-letter word *stop*. Stop sinning. Don't do it any more. Quit. Without this there is no true repentance. And without repentance there can be no forgiveness.

Paul gave a powerful testimony in 2 Corinthians 4:2 in listing things he'd stopped:

- *Degradation,* shameful secret things—Paul's private life matched his public testimony. His walk matched his talk. He refers to things, which if brought to light, would bring shame on the doer. Paul voluntarily gave up the right to do things in private that he could not profess in public (1 Cor. 10:23).
- *Deception,* not walking in deceit—"Deceit" also is translated "cunning" or "trickery." These words carry the idea of purposefully deceiving others concerning your lifestyle. Paul writes that he is not involved in some elaborate scheme to present an impression that doesn't match his inward character (Eph. 5:15–17).
- *Deceit,* distorting God's message—We distort God's message when we doubt it (Gen. 3:1), when we fail to apply it (James 4:17), when we use a double standard (Gal. 5:13), and when we falsely use it to justify sin (Rom. 6:1–2).

Whether our sin is the manner in which we handle God's Word, God's people, God's truth or God's opportunities, the condition of forgiveness remains: "Go, and from now on do not sin any more."

CHAPTER 41

Judas

Matthew 26:47–49; 27:3–5

1. Filling a Great Position Does Not Necessarily Make You a Great Person.

Special privilege does not always equate to special character. Men and women of great quality and integrity, even heroism and greatness, do not suddenly evolve from mediocrity in a crisis. Simply being thrust into the presence or privilege of greatness does not guarantee one's value. Judas was a chosen man who was privileged and honored to live in the inner circle of Jesus, twenty-four hours a day, seven days a week, 365 days a year for three full years. In addition, he was the group's trusted treasurer. Yet he died by suicide—a traitor, a thief, and a hypocrite.

Many people hustle, push, and promote themselves into places of great privilege and influence far beyond their own character and ability to handle the responsibilities. Judas was such a person. President Clinton was such a person—charming, charismatic, brilliant, and attractive, and yet, like Naman, the captain of the Lord's host, a spiritual leper. Morally, the president was a lightweight, impeached for lack of character and integrity consistent with his position. Well has it been said, "The office ought to seek the person, not the person the office." How unfortunate that our political system dictates the contrary!

Good things come to those who wait. Build a life, not a reputation, and you need not seek honor and influence—they will seek you.

With time to grow into his position of trust and responsibility, one wonders if Judas might have become the man he should have been, instead of the man he was. Judas is a mystery. What went through his mind? How could he live so closely to Jesus and not be changed to the good? His political energies were focused on freedom for Israel, but his methods and motives were all wrong. He eventually fell victim to his own lust to be somebody, to do some great thing, and to be recognized.

Years ago, in the Los Angeles Olympics, a group of athletes returning to their hotel were rescued from imminent danger by a policeman who discovered a bomb planted on their bus. As the world celebrated the heroics of the officer, it learned he had planted the bomb himself. Hoping to be the hero, he became the villain. He had expected honor and acclaim. What he got was jeers, rejection, and jail time.

Jesus warns, "He who exalts himself shall be humbled." Our desire for position may well have to do with what we lost. Locked inside each of us is the desire to know again our exalted position in the garden, where once we walked with God. It is called the pride of life.

One day, according to prophetic account, a great deceiver will come. The world will hail him as a deliverer, but his motive will be selfish, and he will bring the world ruin. He will be called Antichrist, Satan in human form. Judas is a biblical picture and precursor of him. The most sobering thing about Antichrist is that he will be "one of us." He is the product of fallen humanity and representative of our self-serving attitudes. Beware what is inside you!

2. Hypocrisy Is the Highest Form of Treason.

No character trait is as sick, sad, and sinful in Christian ministry as disloyalty. In my ministry I have probably employed at least five hundred different staff members. The two most cherished traits? Integrity and loyalty. The two most dishonorable? Hypocrisy and disloyalty. And they are two sides of the same coin, for the disloyal staff member is always to your face, the loyal friend. Listen to a conversation between our Lord and Judas, the slippery-tongued hypocrite, as recorded in Matthew 26:24–25. Jesus had just finished saying, "Woe to that man by whom the Son of Man is betrayed! It would have been better for that man if he had not been born." Judas then asked him, "Surely not I, Rabbi?" And Jesus replied to him, "You have said it." Matthew 26:48–49 tells us that the betrayer had given the chief priests and elders a sign, saying, "The one I kiss, He's the one; arrest him!" It goes on to say, "So he went up to Jesus and said, 'Greetings, Rabbi!'—and kissed Him."

Hypocrisy means "acting out a part." There was actually a time when the word *hypocrite* had a good meaning. The ancient Greeks referred to a stage actor playing a role in a drama as a "fine hypocrite." That sounds strange to our ears because *hypocrite* has come to mean something quite different.

Judas was the consummate hypocrite, in the sense of acting a part. He played the role of a true son of God, though a son of perdition. The curious thing is Jesus knew it all along. Perhaps Jesus used him to set in motion events that would lead to the cross. Or maybe He chose him to represent all humanity and its part in the rejection of the Messiah. We are left to wonder. But we do know this: Judas' act of betrayal ranks as the highest act of treason ever committed. We must be suspect of our own hearts, examining our motives to see if they be God-centered or self-centered. Jeremiah the prophet said, "The heart is deceitful above all things and beyond cure. Who can understand it?" (Jer. 17:9)

Years ago a TWA airliner crashed in Sioux City, Iowa. The cause of the crash was the rupture of all three hydraulic lines by a failed rotor in the plane's rear engine. That spinning rotor came apart in a violent explosion, rendering the plane uncontrollable. The pilot made a valiant effort to gain control and did succeed in saving several lives, yet most passengers perished in a violent rollover at touchdown. A news reporter wrapping up his commentary on the accident wrote, "Though the pilot did everything humanly possible, in the end he could not overcome the betrayal of the failed rotor." Betraying a friend may cause much larger events to spin out of control than the betrayer had planned.

3. The Sinner Finds No True Friendship in His Sin.

Our Lord Jesus would be a friend who sticks closer than a brother to the sinner who forsakes sin to seek Him wholeheartedly. The unrepentant, however, find no real friendship among their own nor with anyone else. How sad the words of the Sanhedrin when Judas, conscience stricken unto death, flung the money at their feet, saying, "I have betrayed innocent blood!" *What is that to us?* they screamed.

Five more devastating words have never been spoken to a sinner, crushed beneath the staggering weight of his own sin. The prodigal found no companionship among the swine, let alone with the bartender, who likely tossed him in the street for an unpaid tab. The penitent thief on the cross found no support from his fellow thief. The loneliest and most foolish person in the world is the man who, ruined by sin, turns to the sin that caused his downfall only to find a "Not Wanted" sign on the door.

After selling his friend for money, Judas burned with remorse. If only he had it to do over! If only someone would understand. Sin begets no fraternity. Criminals know this. They may have associates, cohorts, or accomplices, but no friends. Sin dissolves friendships.

O. J. Simpson has become an outcast in his own country because of the public perception of his complicity in the death of his wife. No one wants him to be their corporate spokesperson anymore. None of the networks have offered him a position as commentator. Timothy McVeigh committed the vilest act of terrorism in America's history. His selfish hope was for admiration and notoriety among his militia friends. But death, not adulation, was his reward.

Sin pays no dividend but death. Expect no friends as a result of sin.

CHAPTER 42

Pilate

John 18:38–40

1. Before You Can Hold the Truth You Have to Be Able to Handle the Truth.

Can you handle the truth? In the classroom setting of one of the *Peanuts* cartoons, it is the first day of school and the students must write an essay about returning to class. In her essay, Lucy wrote, "Vacations are nice, but it's good to get back to school. There is nothing more satisfying or challenging than education and I look forward to a year of expanding knowledge." Needless to say, the teacher was pleased with Lucy and complimented her fine essay. Charlie Brown looks on with dismay. In the final frame, Lucy leans over and whispers to Charlie Brown, "After a while, you learn what sells!" That's a pretty good description of what has happened to our society. The temptation is to say what others want to hear whether it is true or not. Consequently we live in a culture that struggles with believing that there is any such thing as absolute truth.

The Roman procurator examined Jesus and asked Him, "What is truth?" Trained in the finest schools of the Roman judiciary, Pilate conducted his interrogation as a spiritual pygmy, having not the slightest understanding of what he saw. After hours of examination, he asked but one important question, and Jesus remained silent. "What is truth?" Pilate queried. And Jesus just stood there—stood there in a long silence that must have seemed an eternity as He answered

164

him not a word. Jesus in His silence spoke in a decibel level louder than thunder from heaven. By saying nothing, Jesus was really saying, "Sir, you have examined me and you are asking me what is truth. If you don't know truth when you see it, you wouldn't understand it if I tried to explain it to you."

The astounding thing about this phase of the arrest and trial of Jesus is not what Jesus said, but rather what He did not say. The natural man receives not the things of God. God has hidden the deep things from the minds of the carnal and revealed them unto spiritual babes. No one is truly educated who does not know that which can be taught only by the lowly Nazarene. One learns the deep things of God, the important things of life, not in graduate and doctoral classes, but at the feet of Jesus.

A recent Gallup survey asked people to respond to this statement: "There are clear guidelines about what is good or evil that apply to everyone, regardless of their situation." Sixty-three percent of those surveyed could not completely agree with that statement. The search for truth and the struggle with truth are not new issues. Jesus came into a world that was conflicted and dysfunctional, and He spoke these magnificent words, "I am the way, the truth, and the life. No one comes to the Father except through me" (John 14:6). God knew that before you can handle the truth, you have to hold the Truth. Sending His only Son gave the whole world opportunity to hold the Truth in their hearts. Only when you know Him who is the Truth can you truly know the truth. God is ultimate truth, and Jesus came to be the revelation of the Father. So, in Jesus you have the truth about the truth. And when you've got the truth about the truth, you've got the truth.

2. The Pull of the Crowd Is the Pathway to Perdition.

Time and again Pilate sought for a way to release Jesus. Finally, the chant of the crowd, "Crucify Him! Crucify Him!" overpowered Pilate, who threw up his hands in frustration and said, "Do with him as you will." Peer pressure is not limited to adolescence. The pressure to be accepted, to be "in," to be one of the crowd, the desire that psychologists call the "herd instinct," goes far beyond our school years. But Jesus reminded us that broad is the way that leads to destruction. And as meritorious as is the rule of majority in a democracy, the sad fact is that not only is the majority not always right, it is seldom right. Joshua and Caleb teach us that. They were willing to stand against the other ten spies and the children of Israel for what they believed was right, and they did it under the threat of death. The believer is always in the minority. The narrow way is not simply a smaller way alongside the broad way. It is a way that goes upstream and against the crowd inside the broad way. The rationalization of "everybody's doing it," far from being the test of anything of value is, in fact, usually the theme song of hell. The one who would march to the beat of the kingdom of God will always be out of step with this present world system.

"What's everyone going to think of me?" was the question running through Pilate's mind. He was not the first to be so pressured, nor would he be the last. Pilate's decision would cost him something. Our decisions always do. Truth always comes at a high price that hinders those who want to do right. Sometimes I am amazed at how much better unbelievers seem to understand this than do believers. The pull of the crowd was too much for Pilate. He considered the price and determined it was considerably more than he was willing to pay.

3. Our God Will Ultimately Prevail.

Believing means allowing God to change some things in our lives. It means making ourselves accountable to God for our actions. Believing means we are not able to do as the world does. It means not settling for the moral minimum anymore. Believing means that holiness begins to infiltrate our lives. And many of us are like Pilate, and simply do not want that kind of change in our lives.

Little did Pilate know that he was a character in a much bigger drama than the one being played out in a small court-room. For even above the clamor of the barbarous roar of "Crucify Him! Crucify Him!" our Father used the pitiful compromise of a spineless judge to reveal His love for us on an old rugged cross. God always has the last word.

CHAPTER 43

Luke

Luke 1:1–4; Acts 1:1–2

1. To Minister to God's Servants Is to Minister to God Himself.

As a physician, Luke was a special man. In Colossians 4:14, Paul calls Him the "loved physician." I confess, I've always been enamored with doctors. They are, to me, a cut above the average, a special kind of person. But some doctors have callings far above the care of the human body. To minister to the Great Physician, by ministering to His servants, is their ultimate service to God.

Luke was the constant traveling companion of Paul. Surely if anyone needed a doctor on call, it was Paul. Tradition says that he had myopia, an eye disease, and was probably hunchback, needing orthopedic care. That kind of pain takes a tremendous toll on the body and shows in the face. And there was, of course, that physical malady he calls his "thorn in the flesh." Possibly it was malnutrition from isolation and living on the run, colds and pneumonia from spending a day and night shipwrecked in the ocean, skin problems due to exposure and sunburn, digestive difficulties from bad food in prison, wounds from beatings, floggings, and stonings, and countless other problems. By keeping Paul going, Luke ministered to the Great Physician himself and played a crucial part in advancing Paul's ministry.

Too often we suppose that being a preacher is the only real ministry, and all the rest is insignificant. Many churches are held hostage to the pastor-teacher gift, and as the pastor exercises his spiritual gift, the rest of the congregation just sits and listens. But God intends the full range of spiritual gifts to be exercised for the body of Christ to be healthy. The gifts of service and mercy are as essential as the gifts of pastoring and teaching. No doubt Luke had a great gift of service. And he used it to the glory of God and the expansion of His kingdom! I have, in the past month, had contact with two Christian physicians, both of whom felt their great calling from God was to keep those well who minister to the saints and do the work of the ministry. I salute them. They too are beloved physicians, using their spiritual gifts as God intended.

2. Your Role May Change, but You Never Retire from Serving the Master.

We may change our location or vocation and eventually retire from our paid position of employment, but the calling we have received from the Lord lasts as long as God gives us life. The beloved physician begins his letter, which we know as the book of Acts, by recounting what he wrote in the Gospel that bears his name: "I wrote the first narrative, Theophilus, about all that Jesus began to do and teach." Certainly that first narrative, the gospel of Luke, would qualify as a master achievement for any great life work. But now, late in life, Luke gets a second wind and starts again. In Luke he writes of all Jesus began to do and teach; in Acts he writes of what Jesus continued to do and teach through His Holy Spirit.

God has built into the universe the need for rest. He commands us to have a Sabbath rest. When we violate that principle, we suffer for it. There is, however, no such thing as a *spiritual* vacation. It was King David's downfall to allow his sabbatical from the battlefield to become a playtime for temptation. Too many sincere Christians have become little more than pew warmers because they took a spiritual vacation and fell into the Enemy's deception of lukewarm religion. Take a vacation! You need it! But take your Bible with you. And don't let down your guard. Whatever your age. Wherever you go. Whatever you are doing. Remember, you are an extension and an extender of the kingdom of God.

On February 7, 2001, Dale Evans Rogers died at age 88. She became a Christian decades ago, shortly after her marriage to the famous cowboy actor and singer, Roy Rogers. In a radio interview with James Dobson about a year before her death, Dale Evans spoke of her vibrant and growing faith in Christ. She said, "I am more happy than I have ever been. I'm more with it than I have ever been. Jesus is very real!" And she shared her favorite Scripture verse: "I can do all things through Christ who strengthens me." May we all continue to experience the joy of loving Jesus and sharing His love to our very last day on earth!

3. The Rewards of Serving the Master Far Outweigh the Cost.

My life has recently been blessed by some of God's special physicians. Only this week I returned correspondence to Joan and Paul Steinkuller, medical missionaries to Madagascar. Joan is a pediatrician, and Paul is an optometrist. Two days ago I met a young doctor in Tyler, Texas, who was just returning from a two-year orthopedic surgery assignment on the great missionary *Mercy Ship* around the world, who will soon board her again for a second tour of service. Many would think these doctors foolish for the luxury, prestige, income, and possessions they forfeit to serve Jesus. But you are not foolish if you give what you cannot keep to gain what you cannot lose.

Tradition says that Dr. Luke was from Antioch. In the first half of Acts he writes of what Paul was doing. In Acts 16, midway through the book, he begins to write in the first person. "We ran a straight course to Samothrace," he says, and "we were on our way to prayer" (Acts 16:11, 16). Luke had come a long way, over many treacherous miles, leaving his lucrative practice in Antioch, to join Paul in his missionary journeys to Macedonia and beyond. Who wouldn't take the experience of traveling the world, establishing the Christian faith, while he served as the personal physician for Paul, in trade for the most profitable medical practice in the world?

You may think that opportunities like the one Luke had are not available today. That is the farthest thing from the truth! Today there are multitudes of requests for laypeople to come and help in the work of spreading the Gospel among the unreached peoples of the world. Some of these groups actually live in the very same places that Paul and Luke visited. The need is not only for medical personnel, but for builders, computer specialists, well drillers, schoolteachers, administrators, agriculturists, and many other professionals. And no one is too old! I know of a retired physician and his wife who, at seventy-five years of age, are going to China to teach English for a month!

God's reward outweighs the cost you will pay, and God's plan for your life may be much greater than you thought. Are you willing to be available like Dr. Luke? Whether here in the U.S. or somewhere overseas, are you willing to follow God's direction? Pray this simple prayer with me: "Lord, I am yours. Use my spiritual gifts and skills to extend your kingdom. Wherever you lead, I'll go."

Now begin right where you are, doing what God calls you to do.

CHAPTER 44

John the Apostle

John 1:6–8; Mark 3:17; Revelation 1:7–10

1. There Is No True Greatness Without True Humility.

John, the Beloved Apostle, is one of the few undisputed truly great men of all time. And yet, one who studies his writings is impressed that John never names himself. He only identifies himself as "the other disciple" or "the disciple whom Jesus loved." Pride, the original sin, remains the death knell of the human race. John's humility is the antithesis to pride, and may well have been the essential quality of the life of John's Master, our Lord, who is the antidote to sin.

Quintilian, the Roman orator, offered this opinion of John's prologue to the gospel that bears his name: "It is worthy to have been penned in ten foot letters of gold." Yet he who wrote so majestically of the magnificent Christ did not even autograph his masterpiece. The self-promoters slowly fade away, regardless of their temporal and temporary accomplishments. Those worthy of greatness always have about them the attitude of genuine humility.

Humility is not self-deprecation. When we devalue a human life we devalue God's creation. Humility is seeing yourself as God sees you and measuring your character against the character of God. Christ's presence in the apostle John gave him an ability to rightly judge himself.

In a gathering of ministers in Scotland long ago, a young preacher with exceptional oratorical skills was asked to preach. With eagerness, he anticipated his chance to expound

172

upon God's Word. Yet, realizing that he was very young and already prominent among his peers, he began to feel proud. When he was introduced he bounced up the stairs to his task. Then everything went wrong. His presentation was flat and devoid of any blessing of the Spirit. After what seemed like an eternity, he returned slowly to his seat with his head bowed. He had failed his opportunity and he knew it. After a few minutes an old pulpiteer whispered in his ear, "Aye laddie, if you had gone up like you came down, you would have come down like you went up."

Humility enables us to be used by God. Matthew 5:3 records the words of Jesus: "Blessed are the poor in spirit, because the kingdom of heaven is theirs."

Humility can be the perfect paradox, for when you think you have achieved it you've most certainly lost it. And by the way, we wouldn't worry so much about what other people think of us if we knew how seldom they did.

2. The Transforming Power of Christ Reaches Beyond Character to Personality.

Jesus called His disciples from a very diverse and unlikely group of men. He nicknamed James and John "Sons of Thunder." The disciples had no specific educational qualifications, held no special offices, had no particular speaking skills, and had not received theological training. Hot-headed fishermen such as Simon the Zealot and barroom brawlers and back alley fighters like James and John were the warp and woof of the little apostolic band. John would one day write eloquently of God's love from his own great heart of love.

One of my most prized possessions is a stained glass window that portrays John the Beloved Apostle lovingly embracing a lamb. John became the gentle and tender follower of the Shepherd of whose love he often wrote. Jesus not only transformed his character, but calmed his spirit as well, so that his quiet manner could bring us close to the heart of the Great

Shepherd. Personality can be a reflection of character, and Jesus remakes both.

Pastor Gene Smith of Kingsland Baptist Church in Katy, Texas writes, "When we lived in Florida, our chief delight was having an orange tree in our back yard and drinking its fresh juice. But, after a few years the sweetness diminished, and I considered cutting the tree down and removing it. My dilemma, however, was erased one day when I had a chance conversation with a citrus grower. He asked me what I was feeding my tree, and when I said, 'nothing,' he responded, 'Well, there's your problem.' He educated me to understand the sweetness of the fruit is directly related to the content of the soil. If the proper nutrients are there the orange will be sweet." There are some other factors involved, but the principle truth is this: What's underneath will absolutely affect what's on top. It is precisely the same with us. Character is what lies beneath; personality is what shows on top.

Those who are computer literate have a phrase to describe the times when the computation does not reach the desired level. They say, "Garbage in, garbage out." What they mean is, a computer is only as good as its programming. It cannot be expected to perform at a level beyond what it is programmed to do. What is put in will be what comes out.

People behave in a similar way. What goes in is always what comes out. That is why Paul the Apostle warned we should be careful with our programming. In Philippians 4:8 he says, "Whatever is true, whatever is honorable, whatever is just, whatever is pure, whatever is lovely, whatever is commendable—if there is any moral excellence and if there is any praise—dwell on these things."

The brawling, swashbuckling Son of Thunder became the dearest friend of the gentle lamb. Great is the transforming power of Him who can do that in our lives.

3. The Heart Fixed on Jesus Transcends All Earthly Sorrow.

John died the death of a criminal, alone on Patmos. A solitary old man whose only crime was loving Jesus, John died a martyr's death, exiled to a rock pile in the Aegean Sea. And yet on Sunday morning he went to church. Hear his own testimony in Revelation 1:10 as he writes, "I was in the Spirit on the Lord's day." His eyes fixed on Jesus, John saw twelve revelations of the glorified Christ, whom he loved and for whom he would soon give his life. The revelations that filled his life with glory and transcended earthly sorrow and impending death comprise what we call the Revelation of John. If we would die as John, we must live as John. For when He who is *the life* is ours, little can distract or deter.

Any study of John must clearly measure his devotional practice. The time he spent on his knees before God shaped and strengthened his life. The great gift of the Revelation came to us through John's worship. When he was focused on the glory and majesty of God, there came the greatest of all messages the world has yet to experience.

If we had been in the place of the New Testament writers, what would we have written? Paul wrote, "I have learned to be content in whatever circumstances I am" (Phil. 4:11). We might have written to those same Christians at Philippi, "Get down here and get me out of jail." But Paul declared, "My circumstances have turned out for the greater purpose of the gospel."

And what of Peter? According to church history, we know His antagonists hounded him until they eventually hung him upside down on a cross. He wrote these words that stir our hearts: "Blessed be the God and Father of our Lord Jesus Christ. According to His great mercy, He has given us a new birth into a living hope through the resurrection of Jesus Christ from the dead, and into an inheritance that is imperishable, uncorrupted, and unfading, kept in heaven for you, who are being protected by God's power through faith for a salvation that is ready to be revealed in the last time. You rejoice in this, though now for a short time you have had to be distressed by various trials" (1 Pet. 1:3–6).

Perhaps we would we have written something like this: "It's been good but it's been tough! I've sacrificed all the way, and now I'm at the end. I suppose there's no hope for me. Tell the others I hope they fare better than I have." How could they write as they did? The answer is they kept their eyes on the person of Christ.

I was impressed by what Tracey Stewart said in her recent book *Payne Stewart: The Authorized Biography.* She details the death of her husband, golf legend Payne Stewart, in a tragic plane crash: "I still have days when I get discouraged. Sometimes, I get depressed and think, *It's not fair! Millions of people have terrible marriages and are still together, and I had a wonderful husband, and I don't get to spend the rest of my life with him.* On the other hand, I had eighteen wonderful years with Payne, and those years were better than some people experience during their entire lifetime." Tracey Stewart knows Christ's love to be all transcending.

CHAPTER 45

Simon the Sorcerer

Acts 8:9–20

1. Proximity to the Things of God Does Not a Disciple Make.

Simon made a profession of faith, ran with Philip, and lived in the presence of the miraculous, yet appears to be a lost man ensnared in the gall of bitterness and the bond of iniquity. America is filled with millions of young men and women who, in spite of having every chance, are ruining their lives. Born in Christian homes, raised by godly parents, they attended church every Sunday, yet far too often they can't wait to go away to college and be done with it all. Being born in a garage does not make one an automobile. Nor does being born in a Christian home make one a Christian.

The question is, "Was Simon a true believer?" If Simon had ever been redeemed, he was definitely in a carnal state of infancy and immaturity.

However, before we are too hard on Simon, it is important for us to examine our own motives. Do I find more pleasure in the company of Christian friends than with Christ Himself? Am I trying to satisfy some unmet emotional need to be accepted by others, rather than responding to the voice of God? Simon had every chance, but it is questionable whether he ever truly knew Christ.

2. Too Many People Get Caught Up in Signs and Wonders and Miss Jesus.

The miracles performed by the disciples enamored Simon. He had come from the world of the occult where he himself had performed magic feats by the power of Satan, but now he was seeing something far greater. Somehow he was apparently more taken with the signs and wonders intended to point him to Jesus than he was with Jesus Himself. Something like this happened late in the second chapter of John. At the Feast of the Passover in Jerusalem, many believed on His name because of the miracles that He performed. John tells us Jesus did not entrust Himself to them because He looked in their hearts and saw their response was to the excitement and not to Himself.

I am deeply disturbed today about the direction of an entire Christian movement, transcending all denominations, even Catholicism. There is so much right about the charismatics. Unfortunately, more of them will query even their most casual Christian acquaintance with the question, "Have you had the baptism of the Spirit as evidenced by speaking in tongues?" than will ever confront an unbeliever with life's most important question, "Do you know Jesus Christ as your personal Savior?" There is great need for cautious teaching in this area among the leaders of neo-Pentecostalism.

The power of the flesh is never so deceptive as here. Transposing itself into a pseudospiritual key signature, it hides in the miraculous, looking for an experience. The Evil One, who exists to deceive, not only prowls here, but pounces, as well. Remember, truth out of balance can lead to heresy. Spiritual experiences that are sought for the jolt they give play into the sticky palms of fleshly perversion.

Paul warned Timothy to beware of a surface form of godliness. Check your heart and put it on notice you will not run toward the miraculous for a new notch on your spiritual gun. Such a weapon fired from pulpit or pew leaves many wounded and confused soldiers of the cross. Choose, instead, a discerning life in tune with the Spirit of God, asking, "Is this really from you, Jesus?"

3. God's Power Is Not Black Magic.

Have no doubt about it, numbers of devoutly religious people today continue to be deceived. The descendants of Simon the Sorcerer remain among us. Paul warned that even Satan himself would come transformed as an angel of light. Today's prophets and Antichrists are yesterday's sorcerers, witches and astrologers. Science of the mind, Theosophy, Astrology and New Age thinking are just the beginning. Spirit guides do guide. Ouigi boards do lead. Demons are real and mediums presume to commune with the dead, such that even the devoutly religious are deceived.

Simon may even have been sincere in his faith, and could, of course, only speak from the frame of reference of his own recent experience. Simon may well represent that multitude that has come out of spiritual darkness, but not very far. His apparent repentance and request for prayer indicates the possibility of spiritual life for him.

Here is a sobering question. Do we also use the name of Jesus like a magic incantation? When we pray in the name of Jesus, we are agreeing with His purpose and plan, not our own. We should be praying in the same way Jesus did, including praise, thanksgiving, petition, and intercession. To use His name in prayer to further our own agenda, like an ace up our sleeve in a mental poker game with God, is to be guilty of sorcery. Seek God's purpose first. What ever happened to "praying it through"? In a "get it quick and get it now" generation, we are setting ourselves up for subtle deception.

CHAPTER 46

Paul

Acts 9:1–5, 13–15

1. God's Timing Is Never Late, but It Is Sometimes a Little Scary.

The Hebrew Christians had grown so much in numbers that they had taken over the synagogues, and Saul the enforcer headed to Damascus to set things straight. Saul was a scary individual if you were a Christian in the early days of the church. In the minds of the believers, he was definitely Public Enemy Number One. He didn't just dislike Christians, he hated them, and would see them eradicated from the earth. The very mention of his name struck fear to the heart of the early church.

I read a book not long ago with a great title, *God Has Never Failed Me, but He's Sure Scared Me to Death a Few Times!* by Stan Toler and Martha Bolton (Honor Books). Can you identify with that? I believe those early Damascan Christians could have. Saul was on his way, and time was running out. Little could they know how dangerously close they may have been to the end of their lives, and little did they know how perfect God's timing was in sparing them. Certainly some were praying, "Lord, strike him dead." But God had a better way. At that moment, He struck him *alive*—and he became none other than the apostle Paul.

I read recently in *USA Today* these words from Leslie Miller: "When it comes to religion, the USA is a land of believers. A new *USA Today*/CNN/Gallup Poll reveals that

180

96 percent of Americans believe in God." In response to that poll I am reminded of the words of J. I. Packer, who said, "Our expectations with regard to seeing the power of God transforming people's lives are not as high as they should be." Did they ever know how close a call death paid the Damascan believers? Did the Damascan believers ever imagine what God could do, and was at that moment doing in His perfect timing?

Do you really believe the God of Abraham and Isaac, the God of Peter and Matthew, James and John still transforms lives? I do! Our God is the same yesterday, today and forever, and He keeps no earthly timeclock. David prayed, "My times are in your hands; deliver me from my enemies and from those who pursue me" (Ps. 31:15). That's the prayer to pray when we think God is a little late!

2. God Sees the Potential, Not the Predictable.

Saul had a most impressive resume. He was a "Jew's Jew," from the tribe of Benjamin, highly educated and extremely zealous. Righteous in terms of the law, Saul was a Pharisee destined for great success, and as he made his way to Damascus, few would have predicted he would not accomplish his mission of arresting and imprisoning Christians.

I rather doubt that the believers in Damascus stood around talking about the possibilities of what a great missionary and preacher Saul could be if only they could find a way to reach him with the Gospel. In fact, the early church feared him so much that they didn't trust him even after his encounter with Christ on the road to Damascus. Do you know someone of whom you would say, "That man or that woman is simply impossible." If you were making predictions, you would guess they will die and go to hell and create a lot of grief for a lot of people on the way.

Far too often we see only the predictable, while God sees the potential. What could happen if we were to imagine that impossible person as a great witness for Christ, then begin to believe that way and pray that way! Perhaps someone in

Damascus was praying like that for Saul, for something miraculous happened in his life. All I know is that one day Saul found himself on his knees listening to a voice from heaven. What a contrast! Instead of riding into the city carrying a big stick, he finds himself on his knees, then being led into town because he cannot see. Don't ever forget that God is continually calling all men and women to Him and knows exactly what each can become.

3. God's Grace Is Available to All Regardless of Reputation.

How would you have liked to have been Ananias? "Thanks, Lord, I appreciate the assignment of going to the house where Saul is praying. He is probably praying and plotting how he is going to round all of us up and haul us back to Jerusalem in chains. Thanks, God, I'm really excited about this, but perhaps you could get someone else."

Have you ever known anyone who had a deathbed conversion? I have, in fact, been there to pray with some who trusted Christ at the eleventh hour. Admit it or not, most of us struggle with deathbed conversions, especially for those who have lived very evil lives. Somehow, we almost think God shouldn't let them off that easily, and yet His grace is always there, regardless of our past, regardless of our reputation. I think some of the early church must have felt that way about Saul.

Grace! We don't understand it, and we surely don't deserve it. Saul who became Paul understood grace, perhaps better than any, because he was in need of it so much and had come so far. Remember what he wrote his young friend Timothy: "God, who has saved us and called us with a holy calling, not according to our works, but according to His own purpose and grace" (2 Tim. 1:9). It worked for Paul and Timothy, and it will work for you!

CHAPTER 47

Barnabas

Acts 13:1–2

1. True Friendship Never Pushes to Be First.

A true friend will always be self-effacing for your sake. A real friend wants you to be first. Paul the Apostle, here called Saul at the beginning of the story, was a part of the group at Antioch that God sent out with Barnabas. Yet, in this first mention of Barnabas, Paul is not listed. Perhaps the list was representative and not complete, for it does not say, "There was Barnabas, Simeon, Lucias, and Manean," only such men as these or like these. Yet Barnabas is mentioned specifically and Paul only by inference as one of the group. In Acts 13:13, Paul is mentioned and not Barnabas, yet nothing in the narrative even slightly suggests it mattered to either of them. At different times one or the other was apparently prominent. Most times both are mentioned equally, but it appears to have made no difference to them. True friendship is like that.

Godly friends always give credit to others in prominence with pleasure. Willingness to share the reins of leadership and kudos in times of success are confirming signs of a true friend. Unfortunately, we are often like the tumultuous two children riding on the same hobby-horse in front of the grocery store. Jimmy, the larger of the two, says to his friend, "Larry, if one of us would get off, there would be enough room for me!"

A real friend never says, "Enough about me. Let's talk about you. What do you think about me?" Barnabas was not into himself. He was an encourager of others. His name actually means "son of encouragement," and he would, through the power of Jesus, embody his name for generations to come.

2. The Encourager Is God's Special Gift to His Children.

The gift of exhortation, or encouragement, is one of the spiritual gifts. It is not just the preacher in the pulpit who displays this gift, but also a loving friend or counselor who carries our heart's burdens and lifts our spirits, saying, "You can make it. You can do it." The Holy Spirit came to be precisely that to us, and what need we more from our friends than this?

In Acts 13:43, Barnabas encouraged new believers to continue in the grace of God. In Acts 14:21–22, he returned with Paul to three cities visited earlier to build up the disciples they had made and to encourage them. In Acts 15:36, they did the same.

Just before I began dictating these pages I received a call from Craig Julian. Craig is the greatest encourager I know and calls me regularly just to lift my spirits. No one outside my immediate family has ever meant more to my ministry in this way than he.

Perhaps as you read these words you find yourself asking, "Oh God, is there a Barnabas out there for me?" Do you think God cares so little for you? He knows the friendships you need *before* you sense the loneliness and discouragement within! You will not have to look far before the Lord places someone in your path, just as He arranged the friendship of Paul and Barnabas.

The originator of the long-term friendship was probably Barnabas, who was always ready to welcome a new friend. Living with arms wide open is a wonderful trait, and it is especially needed in our impersonal, cynical world. The proverb says, "He who would have friends must show himself friendly."

Cyberspace relationships are far from enough to satisfy or fulfill us. Be there with "skin on" for someone who needs you today! Chat rooms are poor substitutes for real-life relationships. Thank God He doesn't wait until we get online to show us His love! There is someone close who needs your personal touch right now. You may be God's special gift to another who needs you more than you can know.

3. The Friendship of Jesus Strengthens All Other Relationships.

Barnabas and Paul had a great friendship. Their names appear together thirteen times in the book of Acts. At Antioch, however, an argument arose because Barnabas wanted to add John Mark to their party, and Paul did not want him because he had apparently failed them earlier. The rift resulted in the parting of the ways in their ministries. God, however, meant it for good. Barnabas took John Mark and Paul took Silas, and two teams evangelized instead of one.

Note that they did not get discouraged, go home and pout, resign their church membership, or threaten to quit the ministry. The deeper level of their friendship, bound in their mutual friendship with Christ, transcended all that. Through it all, the work expanded and now there were not only Barnabas and John Mark, but Paul and Silas and ultimately Paul and Timothy. God overrules and uses all things to His purpose for those who love Him and deeply desire to make Him known. Their greater friendship with Christ gave stability to their personal friendship, which you may be certain continued strong until death.

Our blessed Lord is not like anyone you have ever known! Earthly friendships are often built on similar directions and interests. When we find ourselves on a new path, friendships often falter and fade, but Jesus will never slip away from you like an evening sunset. Nor will He disappear like the sun in the midst of a storm. He is a friend that sticks closer than a brother.

Friendships are like the popular sport of kayaking. Maintaining balance while seated in a narrow tube is the way to stay dry. Lean too far in one direction or the other and you are sure to experience a fresh baptism. The key is to stay centered with head forward, utilizing the double-oared paddle to propel you gracefully through the water. Your weight, properly balanced, is critical. Let your friendships in life be your paddle, and center your weight fully in Christ. As you do, you'll make great time and enjoy the scenery Jesus gives you. Friendship with Jesus gives balance to friendship with others and brings stability to all of life.

CHAPTER 48

Lydia

Acts 16:12–15

1. God Finds a Way to Touch Those Who Have a Heart for Him.

In the Book of Acts, we discover several characters whom the Bible describes as "God-fearers," who had a longing for the living God but had not yet come to know Him through His Son. The first chapter of Romans reminds us that there is enough of God in nature to make one sense in the heart that there is a creator to whom one is responsible. Just as He did with Cornelius and the Ethiopian eunuch, God finds a way to make Himself known to those who desire Him.

In Philippi there was no synagogue, because there were not enough Jewish males to establish one. The second best option for Sabbath worship was a place of prayer located outside of town, beside a river. On the Sabbath day, Paul and his missionary band found a little sanctuary of prayer outside the city limits of Philippi. Those who had gathered consisted of a handful of women, including one Lydia from Thyatira, who had in her heart a deep-seated hunger to know and worship the one true God. Ignoring the inconveniences of the river, Lydia poured out her soul to the Lord, little knowing on this special morning that she would find Him for whom her heart so longed.

Macedonia lies in the heart of war-torn Bosnia today, and it has for centuries been a demanding society and difficult land. Hardship had always been her way of life, and many

187

obstacles faced Lydia in Philippi just to survive. The difficulties she faced in knowing God, however, were many. The Roman Empire was saturated with cultic worship and a myriad of gods. Prejudice against faiths based on the teaching of one true God was rampant in the Roman Empire, especially in that region of Macedonia. But no obstacle was sufficient to preclude the moving of the Holy Spirit in the heart of this one so hungry to know Him. Our Father does not need buildings and aisles to call the lost to Him. He only requires a heart receptive to His tender plea.

On the special day Paul opened the Gospel to Lydia, she and the other members of her household believed and were baptized. They knelt together beside that river and drank of living water, and her soul was forever satisfied.

2. Service Is the Natural Response of Those Who Know Him.

God led Paul, Silas, Timothy, and Luke to Lydia. Though they were but strangers, she lovingly invited them home, providing a place to stay during their entire missionary sojourn at Philippi. Motivated by her joy in finding the Savior, her home became the base of operations for a missionary thrust that would expand across Europe. Little did she dream how God would use her simple offer of service to Him! Little could she imagine that as the first convert in Europe, her ministry to these men would open an entire continent to the gospel.

3. Small Kindnesses Can Have Eternal Effects.

Lydia left a legacy that shall never fade. Each of us have, as Lydia, been called by the Lord to invest our lives to make a difference throughout eternity. We have been called to present our resources and our lives to the Lord, that He might use them to create a value that outlasts us. Even the simplest gift of kindness can inspire those whom we do not even know, let alone who may not yet even be born. How many mission societies have been formed and how many souls led to Christ because of the inspiration of one good woman?

Paul reminds us that ministry to one another is ministry unto God. To make an eternal impact in the kingdom of God through giving ourselves away is the height of joy! Jesus reminds us that only when we give our life away for His sake do we find it. What do you have to offer Him? Only a few small fish and loaves of bread or a small widow's mite can be blessed by our miraculous Savior to leave a great legacy to unborn millions who will one day walk in our steps.

CHAPTER 49

Aquila and Priscilla

Acts 18:22–26

1. Half a Truth Is No Truth at All.

Apollos was a young man of great potential. An unusually gifted speaker, of great fire and eloquence, he had poured over Scripture and possessed an intricate knowledge of the Old Testament, especially concerning the Messiah's earthly kingdom. His study had drawn him to John the Baptist. He had come to recognize John as Messiah's forerunner and was fervently committed to propagating John's message. He was, however, not aware that Jesus had, in fact, come and died on a cross to set up His kingdom in the human heart.

Though Apollos appeared in Ephesus, preaching with the greatest of intentions, he was the perfect example of Paul's words to the Roman church: "having a zeal for God but not according to knowledge." Apollos was a man of great ability whose message was, nonetheless, incomplete. He was zealous for God, yet did not know Him through His son.

Our world is replete with well-meaning persons who have an enthusiasm for religion but are impervious to any truth of our Lord. Over 96 percent of Americans purport to believe in God, yet our nation is spinning in a downward spiritual and moral spiral. For many, their degeneracy is due to a willful rebellion against a Holy God but for others, it is, as it was for Apollos, due to ignorance. The story of Apollos reminds us to heed God's warning in Hosea 4:6: "My people are destroyed from lack of knowledge." Aquila and Priscilla

190

would be God's instruments to teach Apollos the rest of the story.

2. Much Is Gained When God's People Follow the Prompting of the Holy Spirit.

To continue preaching partial truth was to perpetuate great error. As Aquila and Priscilla heard the eloquence of Apollos and saw the purity of his heart, they were drawn to him. Certainly it was most difficult for these mature believers to graciously and modestly approach this young and flashy evangelist, but in the synagogue that day they determined to help Apollos bring completion to his faith. The Scriptures tell us they "took him home." That phrase does not mean their conversation was at all condescending. It denotes loving and tender confrontation. They unfolded the whole story of Jesus. Imagine the expression on his face as he learned the Messiah had died for the sins of the world! That day, Apollos came to know Christ as Savior because of the faithful and tender witness of two obedient believers. Thank God they spoke to him! How much harm could have been done and confusion created had they not had the courage to obey the Holy Spirit and help Apollos know the full truth of the Good News? There are many around us who need the same.

3. More Grace May Be Required to Receive Correction Than to Give It.

Certainly, Priscilla and Aquila gave their witness that day with love and tact, or the evangelist Apollo never would have received it. For this powerful preacher, too often known for everything but true meekness, to accept correction may have been the greatest accomplishment of his life. What more notable characteristic has Billy Graham than genuine humility? The next time you think of the great evangelists—Sunday, Moody, Appleman, Graham, and others—think also of Apollos.

4. Multiplication Through Discipleship Is God's Method of Reaching the World.

Paul told Timothy in 2 Timothy 2:2 that "What you have heard from me in the presence of many witnesses, commit to faithful men who will be able to teach others also." With that simple command, Paul the Apostle describes the simple plan of discipleship resulting in the development of devoted believers throughout the ages. He presents three generations of believers, beginning with himself. This is the plan established by our Lord as He set the disciples apart, poured His life into them, and released them to multiply themselves throughout the Roman Empire. The result was a world turned upside down for the Gospel.

That principle is beautifully played out in the story of Apollos. Paul had discipled Aquila and Priscilla while they were in Corinth. These two followers of Paul now disciple Apollos. As a result, the completed evangelist follows his heavenly calling to Corinth to disciple the believers there, who come into the kingdom through the witness of Paul. Apollos was building upon Paul's ministry. Paul planted, Apollos watered, and God gave the increase.

5. Protecting Doctrinal Integrity Is More Important Than Hurting Feelings.

Aquila and Priscilla risked much in potentially jeopardizing their friendship and influence with Apollos. But protecting the integrity of the Gospel is far more important than protecting personal relationships. The feelings of others are not to be compared with the purity of the gospel. Should we risk jeopardizing friendships when not doing so may mean the loss of the integrity of the Gospel? Indeed, we should. Many denominational divisions over serious issues have left a trail of broken friendships, and will certainly continue to do so in the future. But the prize is, indeed, worth the price.

Persons like Aquila and Priscilla paid a great price to preserve the purity of the Gospel. We owe them a debt we can never repay.

CHAPTER 50

Timothy

2 Timothy 2:1–2

1. The Power of Christ's Love Exceeds Any Other.

Paul never had a biological son, but he introduces us to his dearly beloved spiritual son, Timothy. In the two letters that follow, it becomes clear that no mere biological relationship could exceed that which he felt for this son in the ministry. Their mutual love for Christ and His kingdom surpassed any human bond earthly paternity could forge. Many of us know what it means to have a deeply mature and spiritual love relationship with another, because Christ's love transcends biological ties.

There is something powerful about God's *agape* love. It is deeper than ever we first imagined and wider than we can take in. Today, the phrase "accountability partner" captures that love relationship with another believer that goes deeper than casual church friendships. On one hand, we are drawn toward others, while on the other, we find ourselves resistant toward yet another hurtful and disappointing relationship. The fear of additional pain drives many into isolation and spiritual loneliness.

However, when we are truly connected to Christ and in tune with His song of love for others, we cannot but help follow the road into even those relationships that may hurt us once again. The power of His love beckons us forward. Charging headlong with reckless abandon, rooted in His *agape* love, we pour our lives into the lives of other fellow

193

pilgrims. Powerful and beautiful is such a transforming relationship.

2. The Greatest Thing the Old Can Give the Young Is Encouragement.

Paul's second letter to Timothy is full of encouragement. "Hold fast," Paul says. He goes on to instruct young Timothy to study hard, endure hardship, preach the Word, and remember what he had learned.

When we are young, we ache with desire to accomplish our dreams. We often run the race as if we are the only ones within the boundaries of the course. Jealousy is often the earmark of self-focused runners within ministry. When maturity rises to the surface, "otherness" does too. No wonder Paul would write that the offices within the church should be for "the training of the saints in the work of the ministry" (Eph. 4:12). The best equippers are those who have been in the battle and know more than mere theory. They have knowledge of bridges out down the road ahead. They recall how lonely it gets during those dark nights of the soul, when they, too, would have lost sight of the prize, had it not been for the encouragement of an elder saint's encouraging words: "I believe in you." As Paul passed his torch to Timothy, so must we equip others through our special encouragement to do the same.

3. The Greatest Way to Honor Your Elders Is to Secure the Continuation of Their Work.

Paul emptied his life into Timothy. Timothy honored Paul and Christ by continuing that which had been faithfully entrusted unto him. Paul writes, "What you have learned from me in the presence of many witnesses, commit to faithful men who will be able to teach others also." Paul invested his life in equipping young men for the ministry: John Mark, Barnabas, Timothy, Silas, Philemon, Titus, and perhaps others. He committed himself to others, who taught others, who ultimately taught us—right down to this present hour.

I have been blessed by the ministry of people preaching on the radio and wondered, "Who blessed them that they might bless me?" To secure the dream and expand the ministry of one who equipped you for ministry is the greatest honor you can bestow upon that person.

The old hymn, "Faith of our Fathers," says it best:

Faith of our fathers! living still
In spite of dungeon, fire and sword,
O how our hearts best beat high with joy
whene'er we hear that glorious word!
Faith of our fathers, holy faith!
We will be true to thee till death!
(F. W. Faber)

4. To Honor One's Heritage Is to Respect Oneself.

Great is the importance of the extended family. Paul reminds Timothy that the flawless faith that was in him was passed down, not in a simple ordination ceremony with the laying on of hands, but in his spiritual heritage that went back for several generations, including his mother Eunice, his grandmother Lois, and certainly many others. We are losing much as we lose the extended nuclear family. Their support and rich heritage contributes an incalculable measure of spiritual wealth to the life and service of great Christian men and women.

Following Pompeii's destruction from the eruption of Mount Vesuvius, thousands were buried in its ruins, locked in various physical positions. Some were seeking refuge from the ash deep within chambers, while some sought protection in the heights of their homes. One figure, a Roman sentinel, stands as a testimony of faithfulness to the end. He was discovered standing at the city gate with weapon in hand. While the earth shook beneath him and the sky darkened with hopeless disaster, he remained at his post.

We carry the call of Christ, the commission of the King of kings, within our very hearts. It is time we live out the faith within in a manner that dignifies and honors those who passed it along to us. May all who come after us find us faithful.

CHAPTER 51

Demas

Philemon 23; Colossians 4:14; 2 Timothy 4:10

On October 25, 1999, Payne Stewart, well-known professional golfer, died in a plane crash. Investigation of the incident showed that as the plane lost cabin pressure, all six aboard the Learjet died. The plane continued to fly on autopilot until it ran out of fuel and crashed. It is a tragedy much like those who work for God but have never really had a relationship with Him. Everything looks fine from the outside, but something is seriously wrong inside. It's just a matter of time until they crash and burn. So it was with Demas.

The case of Demas is a classic study in backsliding. Though we know very little about him, we can easily trace his gradual slipping away from faithful service to Christ. In Philemon 24, Paul refers to Demas as "my coworker" along with Mark, Aristarchus, and Luke. The presence of his name in such company indicates that Paul regarded him as a highly respected servant of Christ.

In Colossians 4:14, however, Paul mentions him only in passing—"and Demas." No fire, no emotion, no sense of honor or gratitude for his service is felt in this simple reference to his name. He is an afterthought. He is just there among the others—"and Demas."

Our final encounter with Demas is in 2 Timothy 4:10. Unfortunately, Paul's final reference to him provides only this sad sound bite: "Demas has deserted me, because he loved this present world." Let's examine three snap shots in the biography of a backslider.

1. A Good Start Is No Guarantee of a Good Finish.

Jesus knew well this principle. I would suppose Judas was as passionate and sincere as the rest of the twelve disciples, an asset to any ministry team. He went out with one of the other disciples when Jesus sent them out two by two. He saw God do great things as he and his partner preached the Gospel and healed the sick. But a good beginning does not a good finish guarantee!

In the parable of the sower, Jesus told the disciples how differently people's hearts would respond to the Word of God. "Those on the rocky soil are those who, when they hear, receive the Word with joy; and these have no firm root; they believe for a while, and in time of temptation fall away" (Luke 8:13). Great start! But a year or so later, they're all through.

The case of Demas should challenge us to take every opportunity to cultivate what God is doing in younger believers around us. Who knows? If Demas had stayed on track, he might have become a great church leader, or have gone as a missionary to an unreached part of the world. While a person's heart is still tender and responsive, invest all you can in his or her life. That son or daughter will soon be gone. Take time to read the Word and pray together. Whether you have children or not, ask the Lord to show you younger believers whom you can encourage. Help them put their roots down deep in the soil of God's Word so they will not only start well, but end well.

Hebrews 3:12–13 says, "Watch out, brothers, so that there won't be in any of you an evil, unbelieving heart that departs from the living God. But encourage each other daily, while it is still called 'today,' so that none of you is hardened by sin's deception." There is in all of us the potential for following the way of Demas. So encourage that young believer! And in the process you will be encouraged. Let's finish well together.

2. Your Work for God Will Not Rise Above Your Walk with God.

". . . and Demas." What a strange statement! He was not yet gone. He was still hard at work among the laborers in the church. But something was not right. Demas was double-minded, and the flaming passion he once had was flickering low. Christians who work for God yet lack a growing love relationship with Jesus are like houses built on the mere sifting sands of human effort. Regardless of apparent success and numbers, there is something tragically wrong. The plane is gradually losing cabin pressure. Demas was busy at work among the faithful, but his own faithlessness would soon expose him.

Like Captain Naaman in the Old Testament, Demas' external appearance was impressive. But take a closer look: Naaman was a leper (2 Kings 5:1). Demas' service did not last long because his relationship with Christ did not run deep. My guess is that just beneath the surface, Demas was making the fatal mistake of attempting to do spiritual service in the power of the flesh. God is pleased only with work for His kingdom done in the power of the Spirit and fueled by a passionate love relationship with Jesus. Failure to do so not only grieves the Father but produces minimal results and usually leads to burnout.

Preachers who depend on sermon books for their Sunday messages may be on a dangerous path. Their people come to worship asking, "Is there any word from the LORD?" (Jer. 37:17). And what do they get? There's nothing inherently wrong in consulting the sermons of master preachers, but I caution my colleagues to use them sparingly. Congregations deserve a fresh word from the Lord born out of the pastor's personal time with God. Beware of the way of Demas!

It's possible that Demas was a victim of "Listen bad" temptation. James describes temptation this way: "But each person is tempted when he is drawn away and enticed by his own evil desires. Then after desire has conceived, it gives birth to sin, and when sin is fully grown, it gives birth to death" (James 1:14).

When we "listen bad," we first listen to the temptations of the flesh. We can only speculate as to what Demas' temptation may have been. Perhaps it was lust. Perhaps he found himself listening to the thought, *How about an intimate relationship with her?*

The next three steps follow soon thereafter:

- B—We believe the lie, the deception of the flesh. "I really think I would be happy in an intimate relationship with her. No one will find out." In our spiritual world something has happened. Deception and belief join together, and sin is conceived.
- A—We act out the sin. Now it moves beyond contemplation to implementation.
- D—We discover death, which is the consequence of our sin. It's the same for Demas or you or me. It is not physical death, but death of a more subtle kind. Death to a tender conscience. Death to sensitivity to the Holy Spirit. Death to usefulness in the kingdom of God.

Do you find yourself falling into the "listen bad" temptation? When temptation first raises its voice, turn away and fill your mind with the truth of God. Read the Word of God. Meditate on it. Believe it. As a result of his affair with Bathsheba, King David learned a mighty lesson. "I have hidden your word in my heart that I might not sin against you" (Ps. 119:11). Put it into action and reap a harvest of blessings! Repent and return to the Lord! You don't have to follow Demas to the lowest level of backsliding.

3. Fruitfulness Depends on Constantly Choosing to Love God Rather Than the World.

"Demas has deserted me, because he loved this present world." Finally, Demas was gone. Paul spares us the details and only tells us that it was the result of loving this present world. John warns us in 1 John 2:15, "Do not love the world or the things that belong to the world. If anyone loves the world, love for the Father is not in him." Demas loved the world, and it pulled him into the black hole of its vortex. He allowed his love for the world to displace his love for God.

We were created to love. If we don't make God the object of our passionate affection, we will find something or someone else to love. This was the focus of Paul's intense concern for the believers at Corinth. He said, in 2 Corinthians 11:3, "But I fear that, as the serpent deceived Eve by his cunning, your minds may be corrupted from a complete and pure devotion to Christ." It is this simple: a love relationship with Christ lays the tracks on which runs the powerful locomotive of Spirit-empowered ministry. Paul's fear proved to be well founded in the case of Demas. The Devil succeeded in drawing his heart away from loving Jesus, and thus rendered him useless for the kingdom.

It is instructive for us to observe that Paul lost Demas and that the Lord Jesus lost Judas. Don't judge yourself too harshly if a person with whom you are working does not finish well. But remember, as long as there is life, there is reason to hope and pray that a prodigal will come home.

In all fairness to Demas, we do not know what ultimately happened to him. It is possible that he turned aside from serving the Lord, but then repented and became a fruitful servant of the kingdom. One thing is certain, however. For this to be the case, Demas would have had to turn away from the world and give his heart fully to loving the Lord Jesus.

Maybe you realize that your problem is not backsliding from a relationship with Christ, but rather that you've never had a relationship with Him in the first place. Today you can begin the most exciting adventure of life! Put your trust in the One who loved you so much He died in your place. And as you walk with Him in a daily love relationship, He will lift you up as on eagles' wings. He will take you through the storms of temptation and the rough weather of trials, if you just keep your heart close to His. He will see that you never lose cabin pressure or run out of fuel before you make it all the way home.